I0106048

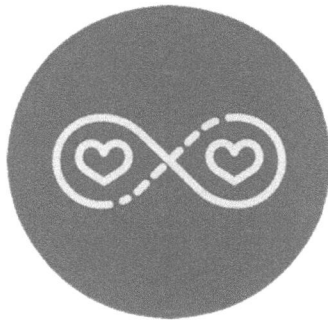

CEEQ, Center for Empathy and
Emotional Intelligence, LLC
Misha Safran
Martinez, CA, 94553
USA

Land Acknowledgement: All land is Indigenous Land.

CEEQ Diversity, Equity, & Inclusion Statements:

All are valued at CEEQ:

All races, genders, cultures, abilities, sexual orientations:
You are valued, heard, accepted, and welcome here.

Copyright @2023 by Misha Safran

All rights reserved, including the right
of reproduction in whole or in part in any form.

Manufactured in the United States of America

Library of Congress-in-Publication Data is available

ISBN: 979-8-218-12834-0

A Teacher's Companion:

How to Center Empathy &
Emotional Well-Being
for Yourself and Your Students

Misha Safran, PCC, MA

▉ What Readers are Saying

"Reading this book is like having a kind wise mentor holding your hand while you discover your own wisdom and personal path. It let me see what is important to me and how my unique style can benefit my students."

~ Kit Irwin, adjunct instructor and graphic recorder

"With a depth of insight that only a seasoned and talented educator can employ, Misha Safran has created a practical tool for every educator who wants to deepen their practice and create meaningful, impactful experiences for their students. You will have a safe haven to laugh, cry, and make sense of this complex endeavor of empowering students and helping them reach their potentials."

~ Vanessa Callaghan, MAEd, parent educator and founder of Raising Our Resilience

"To imbibe Misha Safran's wisdom is akin to having a caring companion and partner whispering in your ear as you engage with your students every day. A Teacher's Companion: How to Center Empathy & Emotional Well-Being for Yourself and Your Students is a practical guide for teachers who strive toward making their classrooms into a community, a place of belonging where true learning happens. The book is a treasure for teachers – and therefore also for their students."

~ Joanna Davenport, artist and art teacher in elementary, middle, and high schools and summer camps for thirty years

Dedication

I dedicate this book to all my students, for your tenacity, curiosity, honesty, sense of humor, trust, vulnerability, and wisdom. All of this and more is what inspired me to enter the classroom each day!

I dedicate this book to the students for whom I wasn't their ideal teacher or who had to be in my classroom as I navigated personal or professional issues poorly. Thank goodness for our resilience. We made it through!

I dedicate this book to new and seasoned teachers all over the world who become teachers for the sheer love of encouraging learners and making a positive difference in their lives regardless of the required content.

I dedicate this book to my parents and grandparents who taught me, by way of words and actions, that to embrace life and all who are on this journey with us, we must accept the responsibility of being life-long learners.

I dedicate this book to my heart-centered life partner whose love for learning personally, interpersonally, academically, and for the sake of social and culture change has been inspirational.

And, last but certainly not least, I dedicate this book to my beautiful children who were, and continue to be, my greatest teachers. You have been wise souls from birth. I truly value your compassionate hearts and clever minds. I love you profoundly more and more each day.

Acknowledgments

I would like to acknowledge my students who spoke up to me respectfully when in disagreement, who stood up for their peers when they felt I said something hurtful, who were curious and chose to enjoy the journey, and who accepted each other and me as our imperfect selves, appreciating our differences rather than blame them.

I acknowledge my colleagues, past and present, whose passion to facilitate learning was far greater than the desire to teach a particular lesson. You were always inspiring examples to me.

I wish also to acknowledge several of my teachers, from elementary through graduate school, who changed the way I saw myself because they believed in me; Miss Harris, Mrs. Trimble, Mme. Schauffler, Sr. Puentes, M. Morris, Sra. Chela, Mr. Bowen, and Mme. Brugerolle. Your patience with and love for me was game changing.

A big thank you to three administrators, Mr. Bob Johnson, Dr. Sharon Brockman, and Mr. Gary Swanson, who supported my out-of-box teaching style.

Several beta readers gave insightful feedback and supported me in the process of writing this book, including my dad (Daniel Safran), my sister (Lisa Safran), my colleague (Nicole Van Rossum Daum), my friend and author of Raise the Room (Eva Jo Meyers), my friend and writing coach (Renee Zukin), and my life partner, (Jodi Lewis).

A big thank you to the parents, former students, previous administrators, and teachers who read my book and provided delightful testimonials, which can be found on the front and back covers as well as just before the dedication.

A special thank you to my editor, Jena Schwartz, and book cover designer, Edward Coronado III.

Finally, I would have likely taken several more years to publish this book had it not been for my dear friend and writing coach, Renee Zukin, and my fabulous life partner, Jodi Lewis. I am grateful for your encouraging and loving presence along this journey.

Contents

Change the way you look at students and the students you look at change.[1]

~ Misha Safran, PCC, MA

---

[1] Adapted from the Wayne Dyer quote, "Change the way you look at things and the things you look at change."

■ Welcome to you...kind-hearted & loving teacher!

First, from one teacher to another, I want to say that I honor and admire you. I applaud your dedication to our future: the world's children.

I also wish to congratulate you on following your heart and living your passion to support young people. Because of educators like you, students around the globe are getting their learning needs met in fun and engaging ways so that their learning feels less like a chore and more like a life-long compelling adventure.

With that said, *my* reason for writing this book is because I have a similar wish *for you*: that your chosen career does not feel like a chore, and instead a desired and compelling adventure which is fun, interesting, and engaging until the last day you teach.

I also hope that teaching will never be a choice you regret. I hope it can be a choice that you look forward to, a choice which brings you smiles, love, and opportunities to empower young people daily while also supporting **your** life-long journey to learn.

Finally, I hope that you will allow this book to give you permission to pause when you otherwise would not have. This pause will benefit not only you but also your students. I hope that you will use this book to deeply reflect on your teaching practices and behaviors, so that you can move in ways which keep the best interests of all involved in your heart and mind. And I hope that the stories and questions in this book support you in trying new things as often as possible.

■ So how can you benefit from the contents of this book?

There are 53 real life teaching anecdotes with questions to help you reflect upon your current teaching practices and experiences.

I encourage you to read one story per week and then throughout the week, use the journaling space to respond to the questions provided. This offers you the opportunity to marinate the concepts you've read and potentially grow in those areas. You may feel while reading a particular experience that it is not relevant to you. However, a few days into the week, something comes up and guess what?! Suddenly, it feels relevant. I invite you to trust the process, be intentional, and take it slow.

The true gift is the power in the pause. Urgency to complete the book and learn everything all at once defeats the purpose of *developing* the masterpiece you are. "Slow and steady wins the race..." This supports longevity and sustainable success.

Wishing you a fabulous career in teaching!

In solidarity and with love,

Misha Safran, PCC, MA
Author, Speaker, Coach, Teacher, Singer

◼ Week 1: Value How You Teach

I love teaching! I love how I do it. I love who I do it for. I want to pass this passion for teaching on to my students. What I didn't know is that I even love teaching ANY subject, not just what I am good at doing!

I was asked to substitute for a middle school math class for a month. "MATH? Oh, no, you must be kidding!" I said. "I am a language teacher; my mind doesn't operate that way." My principal replied, "You know how to teach. You can teach anything. You just need to be a day ahead."

Wow. She was so right. I loved teaching math! And as long as I stayed a day or two ahead, the kids were still learning.

Here's the funny (or not-so-funny part): When I saw those students a year later at the high school where I had a permanent position teaching Spanish (my subject of choice), they told me they learned more math in that one month from me than the entire year.

When I love what I do and value what I teach, I notice that my students do too, even the ones who could honestly care less for the subject matter.

"What do you love about teaching? In what ways do you share these things with your students?"

_____

_____

_____

_____

_____

_____

_____

▌Week 1

Weekly Positivity Chart: Use this chart daily to track your feelings so you get a better idea of what challenges you and what brings you joy. This will support you in changing your habits, nurturing and nourishing yourself, while also improving your impact on your students!

Every morning, I invite you to write down:

One wish you have for yourself today based on a challenge you experienced yesterday.

Every evening, I invite you to write down:

One positive memory from the day in your teaching and/or your personal life that can support you in knowing you are in the right place.

Day 1

AM: _____

PM: _____

Day 2

AM: _____

PM: _____

Day 3

AM: _____

PM: _____

Day 4

AM: _____

PM: _____

Day 5

AM: _____

PM: _____

Day 6

AM: _____

PM: _____

Day 7

AM: _____

PM: _____

Congratulations!
You've completed one week!

Setting your intention for your next week can make a big difference for you and your students!

Envision and describe how you would like to experience this next week.

_____

_____

_____

_____

■ Week 2: Parent Communication

What about those students who are "known" to be troublemakers? The twinge a teacher gets in their body when that one student walks into the classroom on the first day of class, having heard from other teachers the troubles they have "caused"?

Here is where it can all change. You have the opportunity to greet each student with love, greet each student without history, and offer each student a new experience.

What is real and what is not? If you ask for a recommendation to a restaurant, can you truly trust the taste buds of another? It is possible that someone raves about the local burger place but then you go and find nothing you like about it.

Same goes for student reputations. Each student comes in with their own set of history, likes, dislikes, triggers, etc. How do you know that "this" student is going to be "that" student in your classroom? You really don't.

So, what does this have to do with parent communication? For several years, I used the first three weeks of the new academic year to pick up the phone and thank each parent for sharing their student with me and then share one positive thing with them about their student.

The parents of "that" student were in shock. Some even asked me if I had the "right kid". I said I did and proceeded to repeat what I had found to be a strength of their student. These parents were overjoyed. And, almost systematically, "that" student came into my classroom the next day and said, "Thank you for calling my parents. No one has ever called home to tell my parents something nice about me before." My only answer was, "You deserve it!" This was the initiation of cooperation, compassion, and helpful communication.

Would you be willing to take the time to notice the beauty of, and to call the home of, "those" students? If so, what would you like to say? Take a moment to think of three students right now whose parents you would like to surprise with a little praise for their student. You may be delighted to see the difference it makes.

▌Week 2

Weekly Positivity Chart: Use this chart daily to track your feelings so you get a better idea of what challenges you and what brings you joy. This will support you in changing your habits, nurturing and nourishing yourself, while also improving your impact on your students!

Every morning, I invite you to write down:

One wish you have for yourself today based on a challenge you experienced yesterday.

Every evening, I invite you to write down:

One positive memory from the day in your teaching and/or your personal life that can support you in knowing you are in the right place.

Day 1

AM: _____

PM: _____

Day 2

AM: _____

PM: _____

Day 3

AM: _____

PM: _____

Day 4

AM: _____

PM: _____

Day 5

AM: _____

PM: _____

Day 6

AM: _____

PM: _____

Day 7

AM: _____

PM: _____

Congratulations!
You've completed one week!

Setting your intention for your next week can make a big difference for you and your students!

Envision and describe how you would like to experience this next week.

_____

_____

_____

_____

Week 3: Make Every Day Feel Like a New Day

One of the most important things I developed as a young teacher was to invite and encourage myself and my students to begin each day as if it was a new one. Thus, when my students walk into the room, we choose to move through and forward from any previous negative interactions. This doesn't mean we don't talk about issues when they arise, but we both get a fresh start and start anew the next time or day we enter the classroom.

It is the most refreshing feeling to leave yesterday behind and give each other a chance to change, to try again, and to engage in a new opportunity. Every student comes in with something: a bad experience, an exciting moment, not having eaten breakfast, a sibling confrontation, etc. and it is our challenge, especially as educators, to find willingness to let it go enough so that we can focus on the moment in which we are meant to be "now."

This modeling of walking through difficult times and not abandoning someone or holding a grudge against them is one of the best ways to offer unconditional love.

Each day this week, ask yourself, "Am I able to learn from these experiences and offer myself a fresh start?" Then, look at your students and ask yourself, "Am I able to offer them the same opportunity?" Use the journaling space to identify in what ways you can encourage a fresh start.

_____

_____

_____

_____

_____

_____

_____

Week 3

Weekly Positivity Chart: Use this chart daily to track your feelings so you get a better idea of what challenges you and what brings you joy. This will support you in changing your habits, nurturing and nourishing yourself, while also improving your impact on your students!

Every morning, I invite you to write down:
One wish you have for yourself today based on a challenge you experienced yesterday.

Every evening, I invite you to write down:
One positive memory from the day in your teaching and/or your personal life that can support you in knowing you are in the right place.

Day 1
AM: _____
PM: _____

Day 2
AM: _____
PM: _____

Day 3
AM: _____
PM: _____

Day 4
AM: _____
PM: _____

Day 5

AM: _____

PM: _____

Day 6

AM: _____

PM: _____

Day 7

AM: _____

PM: _____

Congratulations!
You've completed one week!

Setting your intention for your next week can make a big difference for you and your students!

Envision and describe how you would like to experience this next week.

_____

_____

_____

_____

◼ Week 4: Organizing with the Students in Mind

Do you know what you want your students to learn by the end of the semester? In other words, have you looked over your curriculum and determined what key concepts your students need to know or understand by the end of the semester or year?

It is important to identify the level of mastery you expect from them in order to map your teaching journey. The destination will not matter if you don't have a plan for how to get there. And you can't create a plan if you don't know exactly what you want your students to know or understand. Sure, not every student is going to get to the same point on the map, but each can be taken further on the path. Having a clear road map is a lot less confusing and leads to more success.

What does it take to create a road map? First, I always encourage taking a deep breath. Some of us are under a lot of pressure to make sure that our students finish reading a novel, a textbook, or a certain number of chapters. I am here to tell you that the true destination is not the end of book and it's not the number of chapters. It's the entire learning journey.

After you've taken your deep breath, schedule three to five 15-minute blocks into your calendar when you can take time to look through the key concepts you want your students to have internalized by the end of the semester or year. Next, create an outline. With this outline, you can pick and choose the content from your resources - don't be afraid to change it up here and there - to match the desired outcomes. Once you have picked your resources, whether it is the textbook, a video, a live person, or even student experiences, you can now create a timeline. What needs to happen and when it should happen?

The last piece is to share this with your students at the beginning, in the middle, and at the end of the semester or year. This gives them some ownership of where they are, where they are headed, and what they have accomplished resulting in less confusion and greater knowledge.

This may not be the way you generally do things and could require you to stretch. And, for some of you, this may be a standard practice. From my experience, students truly benefit from structure and metrics. Anything you are willing to do to offer this can only help them and you.

Outline below the key concepts you are teaching this week and how you will be teaching them.

_____

_____

_____

_____

_____

_____

_____

_____

_____

_____

_____

_____

_____

_____

_____

_____

▌ Week 4

Weekly Positivity Chart: Use this chart daily to track your feelings so you get a better idea of what challenges you and what brings you joy. This will support you in changing your habits, nurturing and nourishing yourself, while also improving your impact on your students!

Every morning, I invite you to write down:

One wish you have for yourself today based on a challenge you experienced yesterday.

Every evening, I invite you to write down:

One positive memory from the day in your teaching and/or your personal life that can support you in knowing you are in the right place.

Day 1

AM: _____

PM: _____

Day 2

AM: _____

PM: _____

Day 3

AM: _____

PM: _____

Day 4

AM: _____

PM: _____

Day 5

AM: _____

PM: _____

Day 6

AM: _____

PM: _____

Day 7

AM: _____

PM: _____

Congratulations!
You've completed one week!

Setting your intention for your next week can make a big difference for you and your students!

Envision and describe how you would like to experience this next week.

_____

_____

_____

_____

◼ Week 5: No Bad Day

So much of this day was hard. One of my students was up and down from their seat constantly, randomly blurting out questions and their frustrations; I had a stack of papers to grade; the administration implemented a new tardy policy which all of the students were grumbling about; my colleague next door had students making a lot of noise causing unrest in my class; I had to lock up three cell phones; a student's mom arrived unannounced; and just as we finally settled into the lesson, there was an earthquake drill!

Because I don't define a day as "bad," I was able to move through it all. But I will admit, I am so thankful that tomorrow will be a brand new day. I will not allow today to define my entire teaching career. Things happen like this from time to time and it is an opportunity to model grace.

I find that as I walk away from this kind of day, it is important for me to remind myself that it is just one day in a WHOLE year and that tomorrow will be an opportunity to experience something new and possibly even wonderful. This is what allows me to ground myself and let it all go! It feels really good.

Are you willing to start over when there have been thankless and challenging experiences in your day? Write about ways in which teaching fulfills you despite the challenges. How can you embrace these positives to support you and your students?

_____

_____

_____

_____

_____

_____

_____

▮ Week 5

Weekly Positivity Chart: Use this chart daily to track your feelings so you get a better idea of what challenges you and what brings you joy. This will support you in changing your habits, nurturing and nourishing yourself, while also improving your impact on your students!

Every morning, I invite you to write down:
One wish you have for yourself today based on a challenge you experienced yesterday.

Every evening, I invite you to write down:
One positive memory from the day in your teaching and/or your personal life that can support you in knowing you are in the right place.

Day 1
AM: _____

PM: _____

Day 2
AM: _____

PM: _____

Day 3
AM: _____

PM: _____

Day 4
AM: _____

PM: _____

Day 5

AM: _____

PM: _____

Day 6

AM: _____

PM: _____

Day 7

AM: _____

PM: _____

Congratulations!
You've completed one week!

Setting your intention for your next week can make a big difference for you and your students!

Envision and describe how you would like to experience this next week.

_____

_____

_____

_____

■ Week 6: Am I In the Right Place?

I chose teaching for a reason and know that I am in the right place every time I step into the classroom. Yet, I still choose to remind myself of this every day. Why do I need to remind myself every day? Because sometimes there are challenging moments such as a parent calling upset about homework, a student hitting another student, five students arriving late, or NO ONE having their materials... you get the idea.

These experiences can obscure my love for teaching and make me question whether I am in the right place. But then my students remind me why I teach – when I see that they have grasped a difficult concept, witness them grow, see them smile, hear their giggles, or get a visit from a student who graduated the year before. And, when I cannot readily see why I am meant to be here in the moment, I look back on past positive teaching moments to reinvigorate my passion. Either way, I can always recall at least one very good reason why I do what I do.

When I keep in my heart, or even write down what it is I love about teaching, challenging moments don't ruin teaching for me because I truly know my purpose for being a teacher.

Why did you choose to teach? What is still true about this for you?

_____

_____

_____

_____

_____

_____

_____

▍Week 6

Weekly Positivity Chart: Use this chart daily to track your feelings so you get a better idea of what challenges you and what brings you joy. This will support you in changing your habits, nurturing and nourishing yourself, while also improving your impact on your students!

Every morning, I invite you to write down:

One wish you have for yourself today based on a challenge you experienced yesterday.

Every evening, I invite you to write down:

One positive memory from the day in your teaching and/or your personal life that can support you in knowing you are in the right place.

Day 1

AM: _____

PM: _____

Day 2

AM: _____

PM: _____

Day 3

AM: _____

PM: _____

Day 4

AM: _____

PM: _____

Day 5

AM: _____

PM: _____

Day 6

AM: _____

PM: _____

Day 7

AM: _____

PM: _____

Congratulations!
You've completed one week!

Setting your intention for your next week can make a big difference for you and your students!

Envision and describe how you would like to experience this next week.

_____

_____

_____

_____

◼ Week 7: Just for Today

Sometimes I feel overwhelmed with the amount of curriculum I need to present by the end of the year. My vision starts to blur when I get all wrapped up in how much material needs to be covered and by when.

Just for today I will attempt to teach what I need to teach and leave the worry of tomorrow aside. I will get through whatever material I am able and acknowledge even the smallest amount of progress.

When we make a conscious decision to be present in today for today, our students often follow our lead. Feeling the release, our students are more apt to relax as well, allowing productivity and learning to increase! What can you do to stay focused on today? And, how can you carry this into this upcoming week?

_____

_____

_____

_____

_____

_____

_____

_____

_____

_____

_____

Week 7

Weekly Positivity Chart: Use this chart daily to track your feelings so you get a better idea of what challenges you and what brings you joy. This will support you in changing your habits, nurturing and nourishing yourself, while also improving your impact on your students!

Every morning, I invite you to write down:

One wish you have for yourself today based on a challenge you experienced yesterday.

Every evening, I invite you to write down:

One positive memory from the day in your teaching and/or your personal life that can support you in knowing you are in the right place.

Day 1

AM: _____

PM: _____

Day 2

AM: _____

PM: _____

Day 3

AM: _____

PM: _____

Day 4

AM: _____

PM: _____

Day 5

AM: _____

PM: _____

Day 6

AM: _____

PM: _____

Day 7

AM: _____

PM: _____

Congratulations!
You've completed one week!

Setting your intention for your next week can make a big difference for you and your students!

Envision and describe how you would like to experience this next week.

_____

_____

_____

_____

■ Week 8: Pause for Compassion

My children and I had a rough start to the day, resulting in all of us running late to get out of the house. By the time I got to school, I was frantic and tired from the rush of the morning. Instead of going straight to work, I chose to sit in my car for a few moments and took three deep breaths. This gave me pause and space to help remind me that my students may have also had that kind of morning. I accepted my own challenge to let go of the morning chaos and mood.

Before your students enter the classroom, pause to think about how they might have experienced their mornings prior to their arrival. It is especially important to have compassion for them; perhaps they were yelled at for waking up late, didn't have any food available for breakfast, their dog passed away the night before, etc. Your compassion for them will make it easier to start their school day. Sometimes this comes in the simple form of just accepting each student where they are today.

Compassion widens the opening to learning.

How can you compassionately support your students this week?

_____

_____

_____

_____

_____

_____

_____

_____

_____

▌Week 8

Weekly Positivity Chart: Use this chart daily to track your feelings so you get a better idea of what challenges you and what brings you joy. This will support you in changing your habits, nurturing and nourishing yourself, while also improving your impact on your students!

Every morning, I invite you to write down:

One wish you have for yourself today based on a challenge you experienced yesterday.

Every evening, I invite you to write down:

One positive memory from the day in your teaching and/or your personal life that can support you in knowing you are in the right place.

Day 1

AM: _____

PM: _____

Day 2

AM: _____

PM: _____

Day 3

AM: _____

PM: _____

Day 4

AM: _____

PM: _____

Day 5

AM: _____

PM: _____

Day 6

AM: _____

PM: _____

Day 7

AM: _____

PM: _____

Congratulations!
You've completed one week!

Setting your intention for your next week can make a big difference for you and your students!

Envision and describe how you would like to experience this next week.

_____

_____

_____

_____

◼ Week 9: I did It!

I feel good...great even. Today started out as a hard day. One of my students was talking incessantly, which was really difficult. However, while students worked on an activity, I invited this particular student into the hallway and started a conversation about mutual respect. They had not even realized they had been disrespecting me and the other students. With a few examples of how to treat others, they quickly caught on. It was amazing to watch their composure change and get it. Not only that, but they also apologized without prompting.

We went back to class and this student became a leader...a positive leader. I didn't get mad. I didn't lose my top. I stayed calm and collected and embraced a teaching moment without shaming them. I did it! What a great feeling for both of us!

There are always a variety of reasons our students act the way they do. Taking the time to explore and show interest in them far beats assumptions and hard-core discipline!

How can you communicate your needs with students without instilling shame?

_____

_____

_____

_____

_____

_____

_____

_____

Week 9

Weekly Positivity Chart: Use this chart daily to track your feelings so you get a better idea of what challenges you and what brings you joy. This will support you in changing your habits, nurturing and nourishing yourself, while also improving your impact on your students!

Every morning, I invite you to write down:

One wish you have for yourself today based on a challenge you experienced yesterday.

Every evening, I invite you to write down:

One positive memory from the day in your teaching and/or your personal life that can support you in knowing you are in the right place.

Day 1

AM: _____

PM: _____

Day 2

AM: _____

PM: _____

Day 3

AM: _____

PM: _____

Day 4

AM: _____

PM: _____

Day 5

AM: _____

PM: _____

Day 6

AM: _____

PM: _____

Day 7

AM: _____

PM: _____

Congratulations!
You've completed one week!

Setting your intention for your next week can make a big difference for you and your students!

Envision and describe how you would like to experience this next week.

_____

_____

_____

_____

■ Week 10: A Compassionate Response

Today a student accidentally spilled water all over some of the papers on my desk. I was instantly frustrated and with a firm tone, immediately told the student to be more careful and to "please clean up the mess."

The student felt badly and apologized. I saw the genuine concern in their eyes and reminded myself it was an accident. And, I saw that they were reacting more to my reaction than the mistake.

I took a deep breath and also apologized. We had a moment to accept and understand that we all make mistakes and that it is okay to feel anger but not to act on it.

This was an opportunity for me to remember that a person is more important than the papers. It was a remarkable exchange of love and compassion.

Approaching students with compassion when they make a mistake or accidentally do something allows them to trust that there is a safe place to grow and change.

How do you react to your students when they make a mistake or even act out in some small way? Do you feel that you support them with love or react to them with anger or frustration? What are ways you can protect the classroom environment to be one of love and learning as opposed to shame and blame?

_____

_____

_____

_____

_____

_____

_____

_____

▌Week 10

Weekly Positivity Chart: Use this chart daily to track your feelings so you get a better idea of what challenges you and what brings you joy. This will support you in changing your habits, nurturing and nourishing yourself, while also improving your impact on your students!

Every morning, I invite you to write down:
One wish you have for yourself today based on a challenge you experienced yesterday.

Every evening, I invite you to write down:
One positive memory from the day in your teaching and/or your personal life that can support you in knowing you are in the right place.

Day 1
AM: _____

PM: _____

Day 2
AM: _____

PM: _____

Day 3
AM: _____

PM: _____

Day 4
AM: _____

PM: _____

Day 5

AM: _____

PM: _____

Day 6

AM: _____

PM: _____

Day 7

AM: _____

PM: _____

Congratulations!
You've completed one week!

Setting your intention for your next week can make a big difference for you and your students!

Envision and describe how you would like to experience this next week.

_____

_____

_____

_____

■ Week 11: Just for Today, I Will Not Worry

Today is my chance to be present, to notice facial expressions, to hear the papers shuffle, and to acknowledge a student who speaks up who has never spoken up before. Today I get to observe, listen, and just be here now.

The more I am mindful, the calmer I feel. This is a gift to all who are near me.

Giving space to be here, now, is an opportunity rarely offered to our students.

In what ways are you willing to model this for your students despite the rush of curriculum that "needs" to be covered?

_____

_____

_____

_____

_____

_____

_____

_____

_____

_____

_____

_____

_____

▌Week 11

Weekly Positivity Chart: Use this chart daily to track your feelings so you get a better idea of what challenges you and what brings you joy. This will support you in changing your habits, nurturing and nourishing yourself, while also improving your impact on your students!

Every morning, I invite you to write down:
One wish you have for yourself today based on a challenge you experienced yesterday.

Every evening, I invite you to write down:
One positive memory from the day in your teaching and/or your personal life that can support you in knowing you are in the right place.

Day 1
AM: _____

PM: _____

Day 2
AM: _____

PM: _____

Day 3
AM: _____

PM: _____

Day 4
AM: _____

PM: _____

Day 5

AM: _____

PM: _____

Day 6

AM: _____

PM: _____

Day 7

AM: _____

PM: _____

Congratulations!
You've completed one week!

Setting your intention for your next week can make a big difference for you and your students!

Envision and describe how you would like to experience this next week.

_____

_____

_____

_____

■ Week 12: Remember the Student in You

Do you remember how you were as a student? Do you remember how your best friend was as a student? If learning came easily to you, do you remember the kids next to you who struggled to learn? If you struggled to learn, do you remember what motivated you to persevere?

When we are able to put ourselves in our student's shoes, even for just a moment, we are creating an opportunity for connection. This connection opens the door for those with different learning styles and experiences to trust you when you offer new ideas which support their learning.

When there is connection, there is learning.

What gets in the way of empathizing with your students? What can you do to change that this week?

_____

_____

_____

_____

_____

_____

_____

_____

_____

_____

▌Week 12

Weekly Positivity Chart: Use this chart daily to track your feelings so you get a better idea of what challenges you and what brings you joy. This will support you in changing your habits, nurturing and nourishing yourself, while also improving your impact on your students!

Every morning, I invite you to write down:

One wish you have for yourself today based on a challenge you experienced yesterday.

Every evening, I invite you to write down:

One positive memory from the day in your teaching and/or your personal life that can support you in knowing you are in the right place.

Day 1

AM: _____

PM: _____

Day 2

AM: _____

PM: _____

Day 3

AM: _____

PM: _____

Day 4

AM: _____

PM: _____

Day 5

AM: _____

PM: _____

Day 6

AM: _____

PM: _____

Day 7

AM: _____

PM: _____

Congratulations!
You've completed one week!

Setting your intention for your next week can make a big difference for you and your students!

Envision and describe how you would like to experience this next week.

_____

_____

_____

_____

■ Week 13: Pause to Listen

We often have a lot of material to cover in one class period. We are expected to cover so much curriculum in a short time span, but sometimes we see that our students are not engaged in the lesson, and we are not making any progress towards the day's objectives.

Sometimes we aren't exactly sure why we and our students are stuck. We learn the greatest lessons when we take the time to pause, move away from the curriculum for a moment, and fully listen to them.

What does listening look like? For me, it's centering all of my attention on the person speaking, not thinking ahead to what I want to say when they are done, not thinking of other questions to ask, nor judging the other person. Listening is just being there, ears and heart open for the other person.

Keeping this definition of listening in mind, sometimes I stop teaching and ask, "How are you all doing today? Are there three people who want to share for two minutes each?" I listen to those three people, sometimes asking, "By a show of hands, who can relate?"

When I acknowledge the difficulty, pain, joy or excitement that may have made it more difficult for students to attend school and concentrate on learning, my students become more invested in their education.

The time you take to listen to your students creates connection, making the rest of the day flow more productively and beautifully. It can also signify a new beginning, diffuse tension, and create an openness which in turn makes learning more likely.

What options do you have to support building interpersonal connections with your students?

_____

_____

_____

_____

▌ Week 13

Weekly Positivity Chart: Use this chart daily to track your feelings so you get a better idea of what challenges you and what brings you joy. This will support you in changing your habits, nurturing and nourishing yourself, while also improving your impact on your students!

Every morning, I invite you to write down:

One wish you have for yourself today based on a challenge you experienced yesterday.

Every evening, I invite you to write down:

One positive memory from the day in your teaching and/or your personal life that can support you in knowing you are in the right place.

Day 1

AM: _____

PM: _____

Day 2

AM: _____

PM: _____

Day 3

AM: _____

PM: _____

Day 4

AM: _____

PM: _____

Day 5

AM: _____

PM: _____

Day 6

AM: _____

PM: _____

Day 7

AM: _____

PM: _____

Congratulations!
You've completed one week!

Setting your intention for your next week can make a big difference for you and your students!

Envision and describe how you would like to experience this next week.

_____

_____

_____

_____

■ Week 14: See Your Students

Today a student walked in my classroom hanging his head low. I asked how he was doing. He looked at me briefly, hung his head low again and kept walking. After class he approached me and told me that none of his teachers seemed to notice him. I asked why he felt that way. He replied, "Because they never talk to me." He then apologized for walking past me without saying a word, adding that he hadn't known what to say because he was surprised that I had actually seen him. He thanked me for caring and acknowledging him. I asked him if he wanted to talk more about what was going on. I was really moved by his response, "Not at the moment, thank you, but just knowing that you knew I was here today made me feel a whole lot better." What a beautiful moment!

All our lives are hectic, and it can be so easy to overlook people and their accomplishments. Your brief acknowledgment may just change a student's life.

What conditions keep you from or encourage you to pause and acknowledge at least one student each day?

_____

_____

_____

_____

_____

_____

_____

_____

_____

Week 14

Weekly Positivity Chart: Use this chart daily to track your feelings so you get a better idea of what challenges you and what brings you joy. This will support you in changing your habits, nurturing and nourishing yourself, while also improving your impact on your students!

Every morning, I invite you to write down:

One wish you have for yourself today based on a challenge you experienced yesterday.

Every evening, I invite you to write down:

One positive memory from the day in your teaching and/or your personal life that can support you in knowing you are in the right place.

Day 1

AM: _____

PM: _____

Day 2

AM: _____

PM: _____

Day 3

AM: _____

PM: _____

Day 4

AM: _____

PM: _____

Day 5

AM: _____

PM: _____

Day 6

AM: _____

PM: _____

Day 7

AM: _____

PM: _____

Congratulations!
You've completed one week!

Setting your intention for your next week can make a big difference for you and your students!

Envision and describe how you would like to experience this next week.

_____

_____

_____

_____

◼ Week 15: This May Be About Me

I had a student who was coming to class in tears. Each time they entered the classroom, they walked quietly whimpering to their desk, wiping their eyes. Once seated, they pulled their materials from their backpack, slowly keeping their head down the entire time.

In times like these, I don't generally ask my students a lot of personal questions. Instead, I simply walk over and let them know I am here if they want to talk. This student seemed to move through their emotions on their own and then started working. But today, they stayed after class and shared with me that they have been depressed and anxious for several weeks and are unsure of what to do.

As I sat and listened, my heart strings were being pulled intensely and I felt tears welling up. Then it got more intense – the elephant was spoken. This student shared that this morning they were having suicidal ideation and were feeling close to creating a plan. In fact, they were going to do something after school but wanted to come to my class.

I felt myself tense up. I could feel the energy shift in my body from calm and loving to fearful and frenetic. I suddenly felt the deep pain associated with agonizing loss. I knew why this was so scary for me; between accidents and suicide, several kids had died over the last few years, some students of mine, some friends of my children. It was very painful to lose them one after another.

Thank goodness, I was aware of this shift in my body and invited the student to take a breath with me. I needed the pause. I needed to slow down my thinking. As a result of this moment of calm breathing we did together, I was able to recenter myself. After talking a little more, the student allowed me to walk with them to the counselor's office, where they were able to develop a protocol for healing.

And the deeper issue? Personally, I have struggled with depression and anxiety since the age of 13. When a student comes to me, which I am grateful they trust me enough to do, it is a reminder that we are all fragile at times and that we each need someone we can trust.

As a seasoned teacher and mother, I have had to learn to take care of my inner wounds and mental health so that I can be of service to my students, my children, and to my community. Sometimes this looks like seeing my own therapist, taking walks, listening to music, journaling my feelings, and pausing to breathe when emotions start to feel intense.

It is very important that you take time to do the same so that you are able to walk through these experiences in a healthy way. We often don't get much warning when students come to us in crisis, so having the tools and practicing them ahead of time is wise.

Here are some questions to ask yourself and journal in the space below: What tools do I have for self-care when I get triggered? Am I responding to the current situation or is there something within my own self that needs healing or attention?

These answers can offer clarity and liberation as well as create space to heal for all involved.

Are you willing to commit to using one of the tools you came up with above for the next couple of weeks? If so, I encourage you to share your commitment with one other person before you start and again when you are done. This is called bookending. This accountability can offer a great assurance for yourself that you will follow through.

_____

_____

_____

_____

_____

_____

_____

Week 15

Weekly Positivity Chart: Use this chart daily to track your feelings so you get a better idea of what challenges you and what brings you joy. This will support you in changing your habits, nurturing and nourishing yourself, while also improving your impact on your students!

Every morning, I invite you to write down:
One wish you have for yourself today based on a challenge you experienced yesterday.

Every evening, I invite you to write down:
One positive memory from the day in your teaching and/or your personal life that can support you in knowing you are in the right place.

Day 1
AM: _____

PM: _____

Day 2
AM: _____

PM: _____

Day 3
AM: _____

PM: _____

Day 4
AM: _____

PM: _____

Day 5

AM: _____

PM: _____

Day 6

AM: _____

PM: _____

Day 7

AM: _____

PM: _____

Congratulations!
You've completed one week!

Setting your intention for your next week can make a big difference for you and your students!

Envision and describe how you would like to experience this next week.

_____

_____

_____

_____

■ Week 16: Laughter Is Good for My Soul

"Laughter is the language of the soul." ~ Pablo Neruda

I have had some pretty funny students who often really get me laughing hard. The best part is that they are appropriate with their humor. I truly enjoy them. In fact, I looked forward to seeing and hearing them daily. There were times when I feared that the humor would get in the way of learning. I soon learned that it was actually a necessary ingredient!

How does the sound of your students' laughter make you feel? How does it feel when you have the opportunity to laugh? Is it something you would like to pause for in your teaching day? What would that look like? What would that feel like? How can you bring more laughter into your personal life and into teaching?

_____

_____

_____

_____

_____

_____

_____

_____

_____

_____

▌Week 16

Weekly Positivity Chart: Use this chart daily to track your feelings so you get a better idea of what challenges you and what brings you joy. This will support you in changing your habits, nurturing and nourishing yourself, while also improving your impact on your students!

Every morning, I invite you to write down:

One wish you have for yourself today based on a challenge you experienced yesterday.

Every evening, I invite you to write down:

One positive memory from the day in your teaching and/or your personal life that can support you in knowing you are in the right place

Day 1

AM: _____

PM: _____

Day 2

AM: _____

PM: _____

Day 3

AM: _____

PM: _____

Day 4

AM: _____

PM: _____

Day 5

AM: _____

PM: _____

Day 6

AM: _____

PM: _____

Day 7

AM: _____

PM: _____

Congratulations!
You've completed one week!

Setting your intention for your next week can make a big difference for you and your students!

Envision and describe how you would like to experience this next week.

_____

_____

_____

_____

■ Week 17: Reality Sinks In

When I first started teaching, I thought that my students chose my class because they wanted to learn the subject I was teaching. I chuckle at this now because it was "news" to me that students might only be taking my subject because it was required. Just because we have experience, a degree, and deep love for our subject matter doesn't mean all of our students are taking our classes for the same goal (speaking a world language fluently, becoming a scientist to cure cancer, becoming a physical fitness coach, etc.).

Even if they aren't interested in your subject, you may be the light they need today and the one they remember for years to come.

This week, can you embrace each learner, willing or not, interested or not, engaged or not? How will you do that? What are some things you can tell yourself to support doing this?

_____

_____

_____

_____

_____

_____

_____

_____

_____

_____

Week 17

Weekly Positivity Chart: Use this chart daily to track your feelings so you get a better idea of what challenges you and what brings you joy. This will support you in changing your habits, nurturing and nourishing yourself, while also improving your impact on your students!

Every morning, I invite you to write down:

One wish you have for yourself today based on a challenge you experienced yesterday.

Every evening, I invite you to write down:

One positive memory from the day in your teaching and/or your personal life that can support you in knowing you are in the right place.

Day 1

AM: _____

PM: _____

Day 2

AM: _____

PM: _____

Day 3

AM: _____

PM: _____

Day 4

AM: _____

PM: _____

Day 5

AM: _____

PM: _____

Day 6

AM: _____

PM: _____

Day 7

AM: _____

PM: _____

Congratulations!
You've completed one week!

Setting your intention for your next week can make a big difference for you and your students!

Envision and describe how you would like to experience this next week.

_____

_____

_____

_____

◾ Week 18: Simplify

It is hard to believe how much we have to cover in such a short period of time. It can be overwhelming to balance the quantity of curriculum with other school requirements: testing, assemblies, parent conferences, safety drills, etc. Given all we have to do as educators, is there a way to keep it simple and feel less overwhelmed?

Here is the deal: When we feel overwhelmed, this creates an open doorway for our students to feel overwhelmed. Yes, there is a lot to cover and even more to teach when it comes to the bigger picture. If we spend time trying to do it all, it just will not happen with great success for the majority of our kids. And there is no easy answer. However, what I do know is that there are two parts to this equation.

First, as educators, we need to take a look from above, so to speak. We ask ourselves the question, what of this material is going to be the most important and make the biggest impact for our students? Once we have determined what material is truly needed, we can teach with discernment so as to lessen the overwhelm that permeates our students.

Second, it is important to prioritize the most important information first.

It is pertinent that we give our students appropriate material, not clutter or fluff. It is equally important that we simplify things in order to alleviate overwhelm for all involved, including ourselves.

What needs to be in your lesson plan this week? What can you take out to create spaciousness? What are you able to remove from the curriculum and still offer a full and rich education?

_____

_____

_____

_____

_____

▎ Week 18

Weekly Positivity Chart: Use this chart daily to track your feelings so you get a better idea of what challenges you and what brings you joy. This will support you in changing your habits, nurturing and nourishing yourself, while also improving your impact on your students!

Every morning, I invite you to write down:

One wish you have for yourself today based on a challenge you experienced yesterday.

Every evening, I invite you to write down:

One positive memory from the day in your teaching and/or your personal life that can support you in knowing you are in the right place.

Day 1

AM: _____

PM: _____

Day 2

AM: _____

PM: _____

Day 3

AM: _____

PM: _____

Day 4

AM: _____

PM: _____

Day 5

AM: _____

PM: _____

Day 6

AM: _____

PM: _____

Day 7

AM: _____

PM: _____

Congratulations!
You've completed one week!

Setting your intention for your next week can make a big difference for you and your students!

Envision and describe how you would like to experience this next week.

_____

_____

_____

_____

Week 19: Preparation Brings Peace

Take a moment to think about your lesson plans. Do you prepare them ahead of time or do you tend to fly off the cuff because you know what you want to cover? How do you feel when you take the time to prepare your lesson plans ahead of time versus flying off the cuff? Is there a feeling that you are capable of last-minute preparation? Or perhaps a sense of calm when you prepare ahead of time? As a teacher, I found myself questioning the need to prepare. After all, if I know what I am teaching, why "waste time" on something I already know? And yet, when I prepared my lessons, I discovered that they were inevitably much more successful for the students!

Why prepare? Because what we are preparing is not actually the content so much as our approach to sharing the content, i.e., how we are going to bring in the information our students need to know. For example, are we using technology, videos, manipulatives, music, written or oral expressions, etc.?

When we share what we know with our students in all the different ways they can receive it, learn it, manipulate it, and practice it, they will retain the material and ultimately possibly even enjoy it.

When our students walk into our classrooms and the lessons are prepared, organized, and structured, our students can feel safe which then creates the container for deeper learning.

What are some reasons you might choose to create lesson plans ahead of time? And, if you choose not to, what consequences do you feel will result, if any? If creating lesson plans in advance is difficult for you, what are some other options to be more prepared for the day?

_____

_____

_____

_____

▌Week 19

Weekly Positivity Chart: Use this chart daily to track your feelings so you get a better idea of what challenges you and what brings you joy. This will support you in changing your habits, nurturing and nourishing yourself, while also improving your impact on your students!

Every morning, I invite you to write down:
One wish you have for yourself today based on a challenge you experienced yesterday.

Every evening, I invite you to write down:
One positive memory from the day in your teaching and/or your personal life that can support you in knowing you are in the right place.

Day 1
AM: _____
PM: _____

Day 2
AM: _____
PM: _____

Day 3
AM: _____
PM: _____

Day 4
AM: _____
PM: _____

Day 5

AM: _____

PM: _____

Day 6

AM: _____

PM: _____

Day 7

AM: _____

PM: _____

Congratulations!
You've completed one week!

Setting your intention for your next week can make a big difference for you and your students!

Envision and describe how you would like to experience this next week.

_____

_____

_____

_____

■ Week 20: Objective Before Objection

Have you ever been in traffic when suddenly a slow-down happened and you couldn't see far enough ahead to know why?

Were you ever in a restaurant waiting for your meal for a longer than usual period of time and the server was nowhere to be found?

Each of these experiences are examples of situations where there is missing information such as, why is there a traffic jam all of a sudden? Why is it taking a long time to receive our food?

People have shared with me that when they are in traffic and they find out why things slowed down, depending on what it is, they relax a bit and may even feel grateful. When they are eating out and the server comes to let them know there will be a delay because they ran out of avocados, they relax a bit and can even better enjoy conversation.

Now, let's put this into the perspective of our classrooms and our students. Have you ever been in a class or workshop and it dawns on you that you are actually not sure what is being taught or why? The title of the class is one thing and what is being taught is another. For some students, this can be extremely unsettling.

What makes your life easier may also make the lives of our students easier. Do you know the objective of the lesson you intend to teach today? Can you articulate that in a way in which your students also know what to expect?

Often, this is the piece that makes teaching and learning come together. If a student isn't spending the entire class period wondering why they are being taught something, they can ease into learning much faster. Yes, the resistance may actually subside also.

Take a few moments with your lesson plans and see if you can identify the objective. If you cannot, this needs to be addressed. If you can, then post it somewhere visible in the room or virtual classroom, as well as telling students at the beginning of class. It's also helpful to get quick feedback so you know they understand. I also encourage you to clearly state the objective aloud for those students who are hearing abled and for those who can read lips

What can you do to clearly present the purpose and intended outcome of this week's lessons in order to thwart students' jumping in with their objections prematurely?

_____

_____

_____

_____

_____

_____

_____

_____

_____

_____

_____

_____

_____

_____

_____

Week 20

Weekly Positivity Chart: Use this chart daily to track your feelings so you get a better idea of what challenges you and what brings you joy. This will support you in changing your habits, nurturing and nourishing yourself, while also improving your impact on your students!

Every morning, I invite you to write down:
One wish you have for yourself today based on a challenge you experienced yesterday.

Every evening, I invite you to write down:
One positive memory from the day in your teaching and/or your personal life that can support you in knowing you are in the right place

Day 1
AM: _____
PM: _____

Day 2
AM: _____
PM: _____

Day 3
AM: _____
PM: _____

Day 4
AM: _____
PM: _____

Day 5

AM: _____

PM: _____

Day 6

AM: _____

PM: _____

Day 7

AM: _____

PM: _____

Congratulations!
You've completed one week!

Setting your intention for your next week can make a big difference for you and your students!

Envision and describe how you would like to experience this next week.

_____

_____

_____

_____

▪ Week 21: A Clean Space

Take a moment to look around your classroom. Perhaps you see a few old torn posters, a pile of ungraded papers on your desk, old projects from last semester. Now think about what your students see and how the classroom space may be affecting their learning.

Some people experience areas which are void of clutter to be most appealing. A clear, clean, and simple space may also increase creativity and efficiency.

Less is more and will offer your students a healthy environment in which they can better focus on their learning.

What stops you from throwing some things away? Could you donate them? Or perhaps ask students to take them home?

_____

_____

_____

_____

_____

_____

_____

_____

_____

_____

_____

_____

▌ Week 21

Weekly Positivity Chart: Use this chart daily to track your feelings so you get a better idea of what challenges you and what brings you joy. This will support you in changing your habits, nurturing and nourishing yourself, while also improving your impact on your students!

Every morning, I invite you to write down:

One wish you have for yourself today based on a challenge you experienced yesterday.

Every evening, I invite you to write down:

One positive memory from the day in your teaching and/or your personal life that can support you in knowing you are in the right place.

Day 1

AM: _____

PM: _____

Day 2

AM: _____

PM: _____

Day 3

AM: _____

PM: _____

Day 4

AM: _____

PM: _____

Day 5

AM: _____

PM: _____

Day 6

AM: _____

PM: _____

Day 7

AM: _____

PM: _____

Congratulations!
You've completed one week!

Setting your intention for your next week can make a big difference for you and your students!

Envision and describe how you would like to experience this next week.

_____

_____

_____

_____

■ Week 22: Remembering My Why

YES, there were days when I questioned why I chose to be a teacher. What was I thinking??!!?

Waking up at 5am after not having gone to bed until midnight because my own kids were sick and unable to sleep. Driving to work an hour early to be sure I had time to make photocopies for the quiz then finding out the copier was malfunctioning, and no one alerted the office staff. Planning my lessons last minute OR even planning my lessons weeks in advance only to find out there was a spontaneous assembly or emergency practice drill. Getting to school early only to have left my classroom keys at home and needing to spend half an hour looking for the custodian or other staff to help me get in. Spending hours making corrections to tests or papers only to find out maybe six out of 37 kids ever read them. Enjoying a student's project only to find out their parents did the whole thing. And the list goes on...

Then, one day at 12:05pm, the lunch bell rang. One of my students walked up to me and asked if she could talk to me. I hadn't eaten breakfast and I was very hungry for lunch, but of course I said yes. While she was talking, another student walked in with a large bouquet of flowers and a card. The two of them, in stereo, said joyfully "Happy International Women's Day!" I melted.

The flowers were stunning. The card was heartfelt. And the two of them shared with me how they witnessed me and admired me as one of the important women in their lives. As I write this, I am getting goosebumps just thinking about the joyful tears I shed in that moment. I had to admit that I had never even heard of this day! Come to find out it was established in 1975.

I didn't go into teaching for the pay. I also didn't go into teaching for the hope of any accolades.

I went into teaching because I had a couple of teachers who made a difference in my life. They treated me with respect even when I wasn't highly academic. I wasn't the perfect student, but I knew they cared about me regardless. They believed in me even when I didn't believe in myself.

I went into teaching to help other students feel they were cared about – and, if possible, teach them a thing or two. I went into teaching to add a little flare to the mundane.

I went into teaching because I LOVED the vacations. Yes, it is okay to admit that!

I also went into teaching because I was good at it. I knew my subject matter and was passionate about it. I wanted to share it in a way students could enjoy it. This wasn't always possible, but I tried.

In any event, when these two students shared with me what they gained from me as one of their teachers, it was the greatest reminder to check in with my why! My WHY is that I love making a positive difference in the lives of our youth.

For the longest time, the card they gave me was what I had posted above my desk because it helped raise me up when I was down. It was a very clear reminder of my biggest reason for being a teacher: supporting students to love themselves and thrive despite a system which could be complicated and constraining!

When I asked people what advice they had for teachers, Yen Verhoeven, learning theorist, teacher advocate, entrepreneur, and mom, gave me such a beautiful response:

"Your Why is your compass. It's your North Star. My biggest piece of advice is to teach to your Why because that's your destiny. Align everything to it, and it will not lead you astray. It will also be your strength, because you're going into a system that will tell you to do everything BUT teach to your Why. Stick to your guns. Oh, and learn how to say 'No' when they ask you to do things that will distract you from your Why."

What is your WHY?

Write down your reasons for teaching. Then, I encourage you to post your reasons somewhere you can see them clearly and often. This is the message you will want to see front and center whenever you have a difficult exchange with an administrator, a colleague, a parent, and especially with a student.

_____

_____

▌Week 22

Weekly Positivity Chart: Use this chart daily to track your feelings so you get a better idea of what challenges you and what brings you joy. This will support you in changing your habits, nurturing and nourishing yourself, while also improving your impact on your students!

Every morning, I invite you to write down:

One wish you have for yourself today based on a challenge you experienced yesterday.

Every evening, I invite you to write down:

One positive memory from the day in your teaching and/or your personal life that can support you in knowing you are in the right place.

Day 1

AM: _____

PM: _____

Day 2

AM: _____

PM: _____

Day 3

AM: _____

PM: _____

Day 4

AM: _____

PM: _____

Day 5

AM: _____

PM: _____

Day 6

AM: _____

PM: _____

Day 7

AM: _____

PM: _____

Congratulations!
You've completed one week!

Setting your intention for your next week can make a big difference for you and your students!

Envision and describe how you would like to experience this next week.

_____

_____

_____

_____

■ Week 23: Model Acceptance of Change

The second semester just started, and I have two new students. A part of me is inwardly groaning because the class has finally formed into a "family" in the sense that we know what to expect from one another, we understand each other, and we value each person's presence for what it is. Two new students entering the classroom mid-year changes the whole dynamic of the class. I know that it will take time to acclimate these students to our "family" and our "family" to them. The most important thing to know is that when I accept change, my students will, too. If I balk at the change, then my students will as well and all of us will suffer from this lack of acceptance. As teachers, we need to be the first to accept these new students and appreciate what they bring.

Even when it appears that our students are not watching us as educators, they really are!

What are things you can do to model accepting change?

_____

_____

_____

_____

_____

_____

_____

_____

_____

_____

▌Week 23

Weekly Positivity Chart: Use this chart daily to track your feelings so you get a better idea of what challenges you and what brings you joy. This will support you in changing your habits, nurturing and nourishing yourself, while also improving your impact on your students!

Every morning, I invite you to write down:
One wish you have for yourself today based on a challenge you experienced yesterday.

Every evening, I invite you to write down:
One positive memory from the day in your teaching and/or your personal life that can support you in knowing you are in the right place.

Day 1
AM: _____

PM: _____

Day 2
AM: _____

PM: _____

Day 3
AM: _____

PM: _____

Day 4
AM: _____

PM: _____

Day 5

AM: _____

PM: _____

Day 6

AM: _____

PM: _____

Day 7

AM: _____

PM: _____

Congratulations!
You've completed one week!

Setting your intention for your next week can make a big difference for you and your students!

Envision and describe how you would like to experience this next week..

_____

_____

_____

_____

■ Week 24: The Dreaded Group Project

In your mind, group projects are designed to get the students interacting with others, learning to collaborate, and benefitting from the opportunity to brainstorm and succeed together.

For students, the reaction may be very different: "Oh no! Not again. I hate group projects!" "Really, do we have to?" "I am always in groups where no one does their part and I get terrible grades because of it! It's not fair." "Ugh. The teacher will probably put me in a group with people who are struggling so it can help their grade or help them learn, but I'll end up doing all the work." "How am I supposed to find time to do a group project with other kids when we all have sports and other things after school? This is so impossible." The list of complaints is endless.

Here's the thing. There is nothing terribly wrong with group projects. In fact, there are a lot of truly great benefits to them. However, I would like to suggest that you first identify your motive and expectations for assigning a group project.

What are your hopes and expectations? Are these realistic? How can you create a group opportunity which adds to your students' knowledge while also supporting the construction of healthy group dynamics? How will you consider the varying personalities and learning styles so that learning happens for everyone and the final grades reflect this in a way which is just?

Below are questions I asked myself when thinking about doing a group project. I highly recommend asking other colleagues, in and out of your institution, about their experiences with group projects and perhaps also brainstorm other questions. In pondering these questions I hope to encourage you to avoid getting into the natural tendency of suggesting that students just "get over it" or that "they are going to need to learn to work with other people so they can just deal with it."

1. Why now?
2. What am I thinking they will accomplish with others that they could not if they were doing it alone?

3. Am I willing to offer some students the opportunity to work alone if group work is really not for them? FYI: 504s and IEPs may actually require you to let them work alone, so you need to be prepared for this.
4. What is the learning objective of this particular project?
5. Do I have a grading rubric?
6. Does my grading take into consideration that naturally there are some students who do very little and some who do a lot of work?
7. How can I involve the students in developing individual and group accountability?
8. How can I support student transparency without causing shame or blame?
9. Am I in a box? If so, how do I think outside the box to make this an assignment which truly fosters learning?

I could certainly go on and on as there are many more questions we can ask. In fact, you probably can already see that almost all of the above questions are significant for any assignment group or individual.

Another idea is to also ask your students for ideas for developing impactful group projects. While I am the teacher and have a lot more experience than my students, their input can be really helpful. If we can find a way to hear and even give weight to their voices, there will be more interest and buy-in.

The one final idea I will offer is setting up a system where each student gets to self-evaluate their process and assign a grade to themselves based on the content they learned and the effort they gave. That way when the final group grade comes out, they can join together to discuss whether everyone deserves the group grade or if some deserve more points than others. Following this discussion, they get to re-assign the points to make it fair based again on actual learning and actual effort.

It has been beautiful to watch my students get into honesty, fairness, and compassion for themselves and for their peers. What's even more exciting is that those who did not apply themselves as much the first time they participated in a group project develop motivation for the next time. They experienced a fair process and they don't want to have to give away their points for lack of productivity nor do they wish for someone who worked hard to get a failing grade.

If considering a group project, what are your concerns? What would you like to try?

_____

_____

_____

_____

_____

_____

_____

_____

_____

_____

_____

_____

_____

_____

_____

Week 24

Weekly Positivity Chart: Use this chart daily to track your feelings so you get a better idea of what challenges you and what brings you joy. This will support you in changing your habits, nurturing and nourishing yourself, while also improving your impact on your students!

Every morning, I invite you to write down:

One wish you have for yourself today based on a challenge you experienced yesterday.

Every evening, I invite you to write down:

One positive memory from the day in your teaching and/or your personal life that can support you in knowing you are in the right place.

Day 1

AM: _____

PM: _____

Day 2

AM: _____

PM: _____

Day 3

AM: _____

PM: _____

Day 4

AM: _____

PM: _____

Day 5

AM: _____

PM: _____

Day 6

AM: _____

PM: _____

Day 7

AM: _____

PM: _____

Congratulations!
You've completed one week!

Setting your intention for your next week can make a big difference for you and your students!

Envision and describe how you would like to experience this next week..

_____

_____

_____

_____

◼ Week 25: Attitude of Gratitude

Today I choose to embrace an "attitude of gratitude." I am choosing to be grateful for each student who walks in and out of my classroom today – in whatever way it may unfold before me.

I can appreciate moments of silence. I can even embrace moments of chaos! I can recognize well thought-out responses. I can honor the rapid-fire questions: How come? Do we have to do this? Do we have homework? When is the test? I can enjoy the smiles I receive and celebrate my students' curiosity.

Today, I have an attitude of gratitude.

Gratitude truly creates a warm feeling inside and out of us. I have found that it is one of the best and most effective offerings we can provide our students and ourselves.

How about you? What are you grateful for today? How can you keep gratitude as the basis of your attitude this week?

_____

_____

_____

_____

_____

_____

_____

_____

_____

_____

▌ Week 25

Weekly Positivity Chart: Use this chart daily to track your feelings so you get a better idea of what challenges you and what brings you joy. This will support you in changing your habits, nurturing and nourishing yourself, while also improving your impact on your students!

Every morning, I invite you to write down:

One wish you have for yourself today based on a challenge you experienced yesterday.

Every evening, I invite you to write down:

One positive memory from the day in your teaching and/or your personal life that can support you in knowing you are in the right place.

Day 1

AM: _____

PM: _____

Day 2

AM: _____

PM: _____

Day 3

AM: _____

PM: _____

Day 4

AM: _____

PM: _____

Day 5

AM: _____

PM: _____

Day 6

AM: _____

PM: _____

Day 7

AM: _____

PM: _____

Congratulations!
You've completed one week!

Setting your intention for your next week can make a big difference for you and your students!

Envision and describe how you would like to experience this next week.

_____

_____

_____

_____

■ Week 26: One Thing at a Time

When we teach, we have a lot to share and our minds are often going a million miles a minute. Our students' minds may or may not be moving that fast. Regardless, when any opportunity to communicate comes our way, my experience has taught me that it is very important to slow things down and not assume that all information has been received nor understood in the way we intended.

This is not because people are dumb. This is not because people innately do not care. This is because we all receive and deliver information in very different ways. If you want your students to understand and be able to apply what you are teaching, it is even more important to slow things down and check in regularly for understanding to avoid losing out on precious learning moments.

"But I don't have time to slow it down. I must teach eight chapters in four months." I hear you. And the truth is, you don't have time **not** to slow things down.

One year, I took a new position teaching French and the students in one of my class periods just were not where they needed to be. I made this discovery about three weeks into the semester. I made a big decision to stop what we were doing and go back to review two chapters of content from the previous year.

Parents and students were up in arms. "What are you doing? Our kids will never get through everything they need." "Why are the other classes so far ahead of us? This isn't fair."

I just had to do it because nothing I could say would convince them more than the results they ended up having. In fact, this particular class period ended up being a chapter ahead of the other classes by May and comprehension was at an all-time high. This was a level three class who were now using French as if they were level four or five.

I didn't know these were the results we would get but I trusted that one thing at a time was more important than the whole kit and kaboodle. It was a gift.

What are some ways you can slow down to support the learning of your students? Perhaps it is as simple as restating the directions for an activity or asking for a student to model the exercise with you before having everyone start.

Week 26

Weekly Positivity Chart: Use this chart daily to track your feelings so you get a better idea of what challenges you and what brings you joy. This will support you in changing your habits, nurturing and nourishing yourself, while also improving your impact on your students!

Every morning, I invite you to write down:
One wish you have for yourself today based on a challenge you experienced yesterday.

Every evening, I invite you to write down:
One positive memory from the day in your teaching and/or your personal life that can support you in knowing you are in the right place.

Day 1
AM: _____

PM: _____

Day 2
AM: _____

PM: _____

Day 3
AM: _____

PM: _____

Day 4
AM: _____

PM: _____

Day 5

AM: _____

PM: _____

Day 6

AM: _____

PM: _____

Day 7

AM: _____

PM: _____

Congratulations!
You've completed one week!

Setting your intention for your next week can make a big difference for you and your students!

Envision and describe how you would like to experience this next week.

_____

_____

_____

_____

■ Week 27: Wisdom Is Our Saving Grace

I first started teaching French as a Graduate Teaching Fellow and my students were from many backgrounds and ages. I was very excited and nervous to be a university instructor. At the end of my very first class, a student approached me and advised me that they would be dropping the class. When I asked why, they said, "I am 65 years old and have been around the world much longer than you have. I don't think there is anything I can learn from you."

Even though my heart was racing, I calmly replied, "I have no doubt that there is a lot I could learn from you! Just one question if you don't mind?"

They consented. So, I asked, "Do you speak French?" They replied, "No." I then asked, "May I share what brought me here?" They consented again. I shared my education and travel experiences, including living in France for a year while attending university there. I noticed a small but sure smile so I added that I knew it was their choice to stay or leave, but that I be honored to have the opportunity to be their teacher and would also look forward to learning more about their life experiences should they choose to continue in the class.

Guess what? They stayed the entire year and it was fabulous ... for both of us!

Moral of the story? Whatever grade level you teach, remember that you are the one with the knowledge of your subject area. Sometimes there may be very little age difference while other times a huge difference between you and your students, but you are the expert in your field. Your acceptance of this fact is key.

Knowing that you have something to share with students regardless of your or their age creates a confidence that permeates and solidifies your credibility.

Take a moment to acknowledge your expertise and journal here about these areas as a way to claim your strengths.

_____

_____

_____

_____

▌Week 27

Weekly Positivity Chart: Use this chart daily to track your feelings so you get a better idea of what challenges you and what brings you joy. This will support you in changing your habits, nurturing and nourishing yourself, while also improving your impact on your students!

Every morning, I invite you to write down:

One wish you have for yourself today based on a challenge you experienced yesterday.

Every evening, I invite you to write down:

One positive memory from the day in your teaching and/or your personal life that can support you in knowing you are in the right place.

Day 1

AM: _____

PM: _____

Day

AM: _____

PM: _____

Day 3

AM: _____

PM: _____

Day 4

AM: _____

PM: _____

Day 5

AM: _____

PM: _____

Day 6

AM: _____

PM: _____

Day 7

AM: _____

PM: _____

Congratulations!
You've completed one week!

Setting your intention for your next week can make a big difference for you and your students!

Envision and describe how you would like to experience this next week.

_____

_____

_____

_____

▪ Week 28: Oh No, Teachers Are Not Perfect?

We are human. We make mistakes. We laugh. We cry. We are not perfect. Sometimes a lesson plan in one class may work wonders while the same lesson plan in another class will completely flop.

We cannot blame ourselves for the change in dynamics from one class to another. We can only learn what works for each class. We can then change our perspective and adapt without expecting ourselves or our students to be perfect.

For example, I once was assigning homework in one of my classes when the students yelped with fear. "We haven't even covered that yet!" several students exclaimed. "How can you give this to us?" I looked at them in surprise and then looked at the pages again and realized that they were right. I had one period of students who was ahead of the rest and I had somehow thought it was this group. So, I took a deep breath and with a smile on my face said, "Oops! I made a mistake. Your homework is actually..." They all sighed in relief, and we moved on. EASY! Had I insisted I was right, it would have gone poorly for sure. There was no need for me to be right in that moment.

It is such a wonderful lesson for students to be able to witness an adult admit to making a mistake without punishment or self-loathing and then...shift with grace. Remember, if you are willing to learn as you go, accept "oopsies" and revise, then the opportunity you offer yourself and your students is the opportunity to fail forward which is so much more rewarding and life changing. You've got this!

What is your experience with being hard on yourself and expecting perfection in all that you do? How do you think that impacts your student?

_____

_____

_____

_____

_____

Week 28

Weekly Positivity Chart: Use this chart daily to track your feelings so you get a better idea of what challenges you and what brings you joy. This will support you in changing your habits, nurturing and nourishing yourself, while also improving your impact on your students!

Every morning, I invite you to write down:

One wish you have for yourself today based on a challenge you experienced yesterday.

Every evening, I invite you to write down:

One positive memory from the day in your teaching and/or your personal life that can support you in knowing you are in the right place.

Day 1

AM: _____

PM: _____

Day 2

AM: _____

PM: _____

Day 3

AM: _____

PM: _____

Day 4

AM: _____

PM: _____

Day 5

AM: _____

PM: _____

Day 6

AM: _____

PM: _____

Day 7

AM: _____

PM: _____

Congratulations!
You've completed one week!

Setting your intention for your next week can make a big difference for you and your students!

Envision and describe how you would like to experience this next week.

_____

_____

_____

_____

■ Week 29: Accepting Our Students Where They Are

Our students don't all start on an equal playing field. They have not all lived the same experiences as their peers. Every student comes to us with their own level of desire, prior knowledge, and life challenges. If we strive to understand and accept this first and foremost, we are immediately fostering an environment which assists in bringing success to the forefront of the education we are offering.

Denying the existence of these differences is more likely to shut down our students, leaving them to feel isolated, rejected, and/or judged.

Conversely, recognizing our students' various backgrounds stimulates interest and compassion. For example, in some cultures, children are raised to not look an elder directly into the eyes. This is seen as a sign of disrespect. In other cultures, looking an elder in the eye is an expectation and not doing so is disrespectful.

What are some ways you can practice seeing and accepting your students? It could be the simple pause and willingness to ask a student how to pronounce their name and do everything you can to remember it for the next time. It could be setting up clear guidelines for how everyone will interact with one another in the classroom.

Teachers are role models. The more we do to learn about our classroom community, the safer everyone feels, and learning can happen.

What do you know or need to know about your students to help cultivate a sense of acceptance in the classroom? How can you acknowledge and appreciate the differences?

_____

_____

_____

_____

Week 29

Weekly Positivity Chart: Use this chart daily to track your feelings so you get a better idea of what challenges you and what brings you joy. This will support you in changing your habits, nurturing and nourishing yourself, while also improving your impact on your students!

Every morning, I invite you to write down:
One wish you have for yourself today based on a challenge you experienced yesterday.

Every evening, I invite you to write down:
One positive memory from the day in your teaching and/or your personal life that can support you in knowing you are in the right place.

Day 1
AM: _____

PM: _____

Day 2
AM: _____

PM: _____

Day 3
AM: _____

PM: _____

Day 4
AM: _____

PM: _____

Day 5

AM: _____

PM: _____

Day 6

AM: _____

PM: _____

Day 7

AM: _____

PM: _____

Congratulations!
You've completed one week!

Setting your intention for your next week can make a big difference for you and your students!

Envision and describe how you would like to experience this next week.

_____

_____

_____

_____

■ Week 30: The Art of Responding

Today, I enthusiastically began my lesson on time. Ten minutes in, the bulb for my digital projector blew out. I took a deep breath and then looked for a spare but found none. I could not reach my department chair. I had two choices: react or respond.

I chose to act with calm and peace of mind. I took another deep breath and changed the lesson plan. I chose to be flexible, instead of reactive and regimented. Was it easy? No. Changing lesson plans, whether adjusting the content or delivery of the content, can be very difficult and unsettling for all involved.

The way we respond to change is fabulous modeling for our students and offers them a healthy learning opportunity as well. It's a win-win!

Do you react or respond? What does changing lesson plans mean to you? How flexible do you feel you are? In what areas do you feel you need to become more flexible?

_____

_____

_____

_____

_____

_____

_____

_____

_____

_____

Week 30

Weekly Positivity Chart: Use this chart daily to track your feelings so you get a better idea of what challenges you and what brings you joy. This will support you in changing your habits, nurturing and nourishing yourself, while also improving your impact on your students!

Every morning, I invite you to write down:
One wish you have for yourself today based on a challenge you experienced yesterday.

Every evening, I invite you to write down:
One positive memory from the day in your teaching and/or your personal life that can support you in knowing you are in the right place.

Day 1
AM: _____
PM: _____

Day 2
AM: _____
PM: _____

Day 3
AM: _____
PM: _____

Day 4
AM: _____
PM: _____

Day 5

AM: _____

PM: _____

Day 6

AM: _____

PM: _____

Day 7

AM: _____

PM: _____

Congratulations!
You've completed one week!

Setting your intention for your next week can make a big difference for you and your students!

Envision and describe how you would like to experience this next week.

_____

_____

_____

_____

■ Week 31: I Ask for Support

Today I arrived at school early hoping to make some photocopies because I didn't have time yesterday. Unfortunately, the machine wasn't working. Then, when I arrived in class, there were a few students who were raucous. I could feel my anxiety rising.

Instead of feeling stuck, I chose to ask for support. I asked the teacher across the hall to take at least one of the difficult students for a short time, which she did graciously. I called the office for help in making my photocopies; they, too, were willing. Did asking for help guarantee I would receive it? No. However, if I hadn't asked, I would never have known what was available to me. I could have ended up sitting in frustration or other emotions, none of which would've helped me or my students be successful.

I am learning to be willing to ask for help. Each step I take to practice using this tool, the easier it gets.

It is not a negative reflection on you as a teacher to ask for help. Rather, it is another opportunity to model to your students how to ask for and possibly receive support. Even adults are allowed to ask for and receive help.

What do you need help with this week? Are you willing to ask for it? If so, who will you ask?

_____

_____

_____

_____

_____

_____

_____

_____

▌ Week 31

Weekly Positivity Chart: Use this chart daily to track your feelings so you get a better idea of what challenges you and what brings you joy. This will support you in changing your habits, nurturing and nourishing yourself, while also improving your impact on your students!

Every morning, I invite you to write down:
One wish you have for yourself today based on a challenge you experienced yesterday.

Every evening, I invite you to write down:
One positive memory from the day in your teaching and/or your personal life that can support you in knowing you are in the right place.

Day 1
AM: _____

PM: _____

Day 2
AM: _____

PM: _____

Day 3
AM: _____

PM: _____

Day 4
AM: _____

PM: _____

Day 5

AM: _____

PM: _____

Day 6

AM: _____

PM: _____

Day 7

AM: _____

PM: _____

Congratulations!
You've completed one week!

Setting your intention for your next week can make a big difference for you and your students!

Envision and describe how you would like to experience this next week.

_____

_____

_____

_____

■ Week 32: I Can Do This

180 students, 80 exams and 100 papers to grade, two IEP (individual education plan) meetings, three SST (Student Study Team) meetings, one staff meeting and a department meeting (and a partridge in a pear tree ha-ha). An extremely busy week!

The tasks add up quickly and resolve slowly. But I can do this, one task at a time. If I focus on one item on my list without allowing my brain to jump to the next item just for the sole purpose of stressing myself out, I will be more successful and efficient.

Sometimes committing to doing life imperfectly really helps. Other times, it's about choosing one task and starting on it, even if only for 20 minutes. The best part is knowing that we will not allow this busy week to overwhelm us... it will subside as we chip away one task at a time.

In overscheduled weeks like these, what are some ways to take care of yourself? Use the space below to do some brainstorming and planning for this week in order to gain a clearer picture of when it is possible to integrate your self-care.

_____

_____

_____

_____

_____

_____

_____

_____

_____

Week 32

Weekly Positivity Chart: Use this chart daily to track your feelings so you get a better idea of what challenges you and what brings you joy. This will support you in changing your habits, nurturing and nourishing yourself, while also improving your impact on your students!

Every morning, I invite you to write down:

One wish you have for yourself today based on a challenge you experienced yesterday.

Every evening, I invite you to write down:

One positive memory from the day in your teaching and/or your personal life that can support you in knowing you are in the right place.

Day 1

AM: _____

PM: _____

Day 2

AM: _____

PM: _____

Day 3

AM: _____

PM: _____

Day 4

AM: _____

PM: _____

Day 5

AM: _____

PM: _____

Day 6

AM: _____

PM: _____

Day 7

AM: _____

PM: _____

Congratulations!
You've completed one week!

Setting your intention for your next week can make a big difference for you and your students!

Envision and describe how you would like to experience this next week.

_____

_____

_____

_____

Week 33: There Is an Assembly Today?

My school has a communication problem, resulting in many of us finding out at the last minute about rallies, practice drills, meetings and/or assemblies. Today I was so proud of the time I took to create my lesson plans in order to cover the necessary material before state testing next week. Then I found out at the last minute that there was an assembly. WHAT? So, what did I do instead of complaining or reacting negatively to the news? Besides breathing, I quickly thought outside of the box and shifted my lesson plan to involve the assembly.

Instead of my original writing project planned for the class, I had my students take mental notes during the assembly so that when we returned to the classroom, they could write a news report about what they learned. This turned out to be even better than what was originally planned. Their news reports were fun, interesting, and creative! The students also got more out of that assembly than many prior ones because they were attentive, looking for ideas to latch onto so they could do well on the assignment.

Your students will benefit one way or another from your guidance and flexibility. It is through watching you shift gracefully that gives them the gifts of calm, safety, and willingness to do the same.

Are you willing to go with the flow? What might that look like for you?

_____

_____

_____

_____

_____

_____

_____

_____

Week 33

Weekly Positivity Chart: Use this chart daily to track your feelings so you get a better idea of what challenges you and what brings you joy. This will support you in changing your habits, nurturing and nourishing yourself, while also improving your impact on your students!

Every morning, I invite you to write down:

One wish you have for yourself today based on a challenge you experienced yesterday.

Every evening, I invite you to write down:

One positive memory from the day in your teaching and/or your personal life that can support you in knowing you are in the right place.

Day 1

AM: _____

PM: _____

Day 2

AM: _____

PM: _____

Day 3

AM: _____

PM: _____

Day 4

AM: _____

PM: _____

Day 5

AM: _____

PM: _____

Day 6

AM: _____

PM: _____

Day 7

AM: _____

PM: _____

Congratulations!
You've completed one week!

Setting your intention for your next week can make a big difference for you and your students!

Envision and describe how you would like to experience this next week.

_____

_____

_____

_____

◼ Week 34: Fake it 'til You Make It

Sometimes we have to fake it 'til we make it. Even if we are feeling down, exhausted, and/or overwhelmed, we can model to our students that we can walk through the discomfort one hour at a time or sometimes 10 minutes at a time.

Know that the more positive energy you possess, the more it will flow outward to your students. Your students will appreciate that first smile of their day. You may also find that it brings you peace and contentment. Faking it 'til You Make It becomes a catalyst for emotional regulation...what a gift!

Try this: Set a timer for one minute. Look in the mirror and smile really big at yourself for the entire minute...YES, a whole minute! Really look at your smile while thinking positive thoughts.

What came up for you? Did you end up laughing? Did your smile start to feel real? What could be the value of doing this every time you feel overwhelmed?

_____

_____

_____

_____

_____

_____

_____

_____

_____

Week 34

Weekly Positivity Chart: Use this chart daily to track your feelings so you get a better idea of what challenges you and what brings you joy. This will support you in changing your habits, nurturing and nourishing yourself, while also improving your impact on your students!

Every morning, I invite you to write down:

One wish you have for yourself today based on a challenge you experienced yesterday.

Every evening, I invite you to write down:

One positive memory from the day in your teaching and/or your personal life that can support you in knowing you are in the right place.

Day 1

AM: _____

PM: _____

Day 2

AM: _____

PM: _____

Day 3

AM: _____

PM: _____

Day 4

AM: _____

PM: _____

Day 5

AM: _____

PM: _____

Day 6

AM: _____

PM: _____

Day 7

AM: _____

PM: _____

Congratulations!
You've completed one week!

Setting your intention for your next week can make a big difference for you and your students!

Envision and describe how you would like to experience this next week.

_____

_____

_____

_____

■ Week 35: Think Before I Speak

The reality is that it is often an additional burden when an adult shares their feelings with their students when it is for anything other than for the purpose of modeling sensitivity and empathy. We are adults. While many students are mature, we have no way of knowing how our personal information will land for them. I learned this the hard way.

One day, while teaching adjectives in French, I used humor about my divorce. While many of the students were entertained, one of my students, whose parents were going through a very painful divorce, was very upset by it. When I learned this, I truly felt awful. Though it was good for me to laugh about the process, it wasn't good for her – and possibly others who didn't have the courage to speak up. I was fortunate that she was willing to share with me how this impacted her.

Our experiences are important and even helpful if shared in a neutral way. And it is critical that we use discernment. A student can easily begin to attach to our feelings because they care about us or not share how they feel because they don't want to offend or disappoint us. It is important to think before we speak and pay attention to how our stories and experiences might impact our students. When preparing examples for class discussion or student engagement, consider that there is a huge variety of experiences in the room.

Do you take time to learn about the different students you have in your classes? What information could you ask for to help you maximize your effect on their learning? What stories and experiences can you share that could enhance student learning? What stories might negatively impact learning?

_____

_____

_____

_____

_____

_____

Week 35

Weekly Positivity Chart: Use this chart daily to track your feelings so you get a better idea of what challenges you and what brings you joy. This will support you in changing your habits, nurturing and nourishing yourself, while also improving your impact on your students!

Every morning, I invite you to write down:
One wish you have for yourself today based on a challenge you experienced yesterday.

Every evening, I invite you to write down:
One positive memory from the day in your teaching and/or your personal life that can support you in knowing you are in the right place.

Day 1
AM: _____
PM: _____

Day 2
AM: _____
PM: _____

Day 3
AM: _____
PM: _____

Day 4
AM: _____
PM: _____

Day 5

AM: _____

PM: _____

Day 6

AM: _____

PM: _____

Day 7

AM: _____

PM: _____

Congratulations!
You've completed one week!

Setting your intention for your next week can make a big difference for you and your students!

Envision and describe how you would like to experience this next week.

_____

_____

_____

_____

■ Week 36: Patience and Photocopy Machines

When I give a test in my class, I have to make copies of the blank answer sheet template in order for students to take the exam. Often there are grids or charts and/or pictures as well, so using a simple sheet of paper doesn't work well and even causes more confusion for the students (not to mention it makes them much harder to grade).

The copy machine breaking down definitely causes a bigger challenge for testing. It could potentially derail me. In these moments, I remember that I have two choices: Get flustered and panic or breathe and come up with a solution.

Today I will breathe and come up with a solution. Note to self: I waited too long to make the copies because I was very busy, so it is up to me to come up with another workable plan. We will take half of the exam today for which they can use a normal piece of paper and hope for a repaired machine soon so we can complete the other areas of the exam another day.

This solution is better than nothing. It provides me with some peace of mind as well as a beginning point which I can use to assess the students. I can also pass on my calm energy to my students. It is a two-fold lesson for me: don't wait until the last minute and definitely don't put my mistake onto my students.

As my students witness my willingness to be patient and flexible, they naturally relax and move with me as opposed to against me. Additionally, they are getting to see resilience in action.

Have you experienced last-minute "fails"? If so, how do you move through these with grace? If not, what can you do to support yourself when this happens?

_____

_____

_____

_____

Week 36

Weekly Positivity Chart: Use this chart daily to track your feelings so you get a better idea of what challenges you and what brings you joy. This will support you in changing your habits, nurturing and nourishing yourself, while also improving your impact on your students!

Every morning, I invite you to write down:

One wish you have for yourself today based on a challenge you experienced yesterday.

Every evening, I invite you to write down:

One positive memory from the day in your teaching and/or your personal life that can support you in knowing you are in the right place.

Day 1

AM: _____

PM: _____

Day 2

AM: _____

PM: _____

Day 3

AM: _____

PM: _____

Day 4

AM: _____

PM: _____

Day 5

AM: _____

PM: _____

Day 6

AM: _____

PM: _____

Day 7

AM: _____

PM: _____

Congratulations!
You've completed one week!

Setting your intention for your next week can make a big difference for you and your students!

Envision and describe how you would like to experience this next week..

_____

_____

_____

_____

■ Week 37: Pockets of Peace

I took a few extra minutes before leaving the classroom yesterday to prepare my lessons, write on the white board, and make the necessary copies. I walked into class this morning and felt prepared and ready to go. How great it feels. My energy will permeate, and it will be a good day.

Taking a short 15-30 minutes to prepare ahead brings space for calmness.

What does peace feel like to you? How could this impact those around you? What are a few smaller steps you can take today for a peaceful tomorrow or week?

_____

_____

_____

_____

_____

_____

_____

_____

_____

_____

_____

_____

▌ Week 37

Weekly Positivity Chart: Use this chart daily to track your feelings so you get a better idea of what challenges you and what brings you joy. This will support you in changing your habits, nurturing and nourishing yourself, while also improving your impact on your students!

Every morning, I invite you to write down:
One wish you have for yourself today based on a challenge you experienced yesterday.

Every evening, I invite you to write down:
One positive memory from the day in your teaching and/or your personal life that can support you in knowing you are in the right place.

Day 1
AM: _____
PM: _____

Day 2
AM: _____
PM: _____

Day 3
AM: _____
PM: _____

Day 4
AM: _____
PM: _____

Day 5

AM: _____

PM: _____

Day 6

AM: _____

PM: _____

Day 7

AM: _____

PM: _____

Congratulations!
You've completed one week!

Setting your intention for your next week can make a big difference for you and your students!

Envision and describe how you would like to experience this next week.

_____

_____

_____

_____

Week 38: I Focus on My Students

I got up after a long, sleepless night. There were numerous things going on in my personal life which were flooding my thoughts. On my way to school, I made a decision to meditate and actively participate in a mind shift. When I got to school, I opened my classroom door and began my preparation for the day. It was clear to me that a weight had dropped off my shoulders. I was surprised to feel relieved of my personal challenges and ready to focus on my students.

As the first student walked into the room, I noticed the joy flowing into my heart. With each new face, I was relieved of my own angst and a new thought came over me. What about their troubles?

We all have personal issues from one day to another and at school, my focus is on my students. When I leave the classroom today, I can go back to thinking about my personal life and use the tools I have gained to practice my self-care. This was a big ah-ha and gave me much clarity for days to come.

Have you noticed that our students have to do this every day?

They come to school with multiple concerns, pains and fears, and yet many of them leave these feelings and experiences at the door. They may share with friends during the breaks but they come into the classroom and most often focus on the tasks at hand. Putting our focus on our students is another reason for them to feel safe and cared for.

What clarity has this provided you today? How can you use this as you walk into your next workdays?

_____

_____

_____

_____

_____

_____

▌Week 38

Weekly Positivity Chart: Use this chart daily to track your feelings so you get a better idea of what challenges you and what brings you joy. This will support you in changing your habits, nurturing and nourishing yourself, while also improving your impact on your students!

Every morning, I invite you to write down:

One wish you have for yourself today based on a challenge you experienced yesterday.

Every evening, I invite you to write down:

One positive memory from the day in your teaching and/or your personal life that can support you in knowing you are in the right place.

Day 1

AM: _____

PM: _____

Day 2

AM: _____

PM: _____

Day 3

AM: _____

PM: _____

Day 4

AM: _____

PM: _____

Day 5

AM: _____

PM: _____

Day 6

AM: _____

PM: _____

Day 7

AM: _____

PM: _____

Congratulations!
You've completed one week!

Setting your intention for your next week can make a big difference for you and your students!

Envision and describe how you would like to experience this next week.

_____

_____

_____

_____

■ Week 39: I Am an Imperfect Perfectionist with Expectations!

I used to have this idea that I always had to be perfect at everything I did. As a result, my students felt pressured to be the same way. This was a very unhealthy expectation of myself and them.

Some may argue that striving for perfection can assist in keeping up one's motivation. However, it also can create a lot of stress and anxiety. I've often exerted myself to the point of exhaustion. When the pressure is reduced and students have room to explore they are more likely to learn.

I found that letting go of my need to be perfect doesn't change the outcome; rather, it allows me and my students to attain the same, if not better, academic results.

Once we have identified our expectations it may be helpful to evaluate what is the most important piece for this journey today. How can you be flexible and gentle with yourselves and your students this week?

In what areas are you perhaps expecting too much for yourself? For your students? Where can you release some pressure? How do these expectations impact your teaching? Your students' ability to learn?

_____

_____

_____

_____

_____

_____

_____

_____

Week 39

Weekly Positivity Chart: Use this chart daily to track your feelings so you get a better idea of what challenges you and what brings you joy. This will support you in changing your habits, nurturing and nourishing yourself, while also improving your impact on your students!

Every morning, I invite you to write down:

One wish you have for yourself today based on a challenge you experienced yesterday.

Every evening, I invite you to write down:

One positive memory from the day in your teaching and/or your personal life that can support you in knowing you are in the right place.

Day 1

AM: _____

PM: _____

Day 2

AM: _____

PM: _____

Day 3

AM: _____

PM: _____

Day 4

AM: _____

PM: _____

Day 5

AM: _____

PM: _____

Day 6

AM: _____

PM: _____

Day 7

AM: _____

PM: _____

Congratulations!
You've completed one week!

Setting your intention for your next week can make a big difference for you and your students!

Envision and describe how you would like to experience this next week.

_____

_____

_____

_____

■ Week 40: I Let Go

Today I feel anxious. I am anxious about my ability to provide a great lesson and motivate the unmotivated.

I often feel responsible for the academic success of each student, thus putting undue pressure on myself. Today I will let go and release some of the responsibility back to my students. They have a choice to learn. It is their choice whether to participate, seek to learn, to use the tools I am teaching them, etc.

My job as the teacher is to teach, to create an engaging environment, and to provide skills. My students' job is to learn. I cannot force the learning to happen. There is only so much I can do if they choose to be on their phones, leave their books in their lockers or at home, or talk instead of take notes.

Oftentimes the progressive model of teaching puts too much pressure on teachers to entertain and do for our students what they can do for themselves. Students need to learn accountability for their lives and their education is one important facet of this.

What tasks do not belong to you that you are willing to let go of this week? What does letting go look like? What support do you need to make sure this happens?

_____

_____

_____

_____

_____

_____

_____

Week 40

Weekly Positivity Chart: Use this chart daily to track your feelings so you get a better idea of what challenges you and what brings you joy. This will support you in changing your habits, nurturing and nourishing yourself, while also improving your impact on your students!

Every morning, I invite you to write down:

One wish you have for yourself today based on a challenge you experienced yesterday.

Every evening, I invite you to write down:

One positive memory from the day in your teaching and/or your personal life that can support you in knowing you are in the right place.

Day 1

AM: _____

PM: _____

Day 2

AM: _____

PM: _____

Day 3

AM: _____

PM: _____

Day 4

AM: _____

PM: _____

Day 5

AM: _____

PM: _____

Day 6

AM: _____

PM: _____

Day 7

AM: _____

PM: _____

Congratulations!
You've completed one week!

Setting your intention for your next week can make a big difference for you and your students!

Envision and describe how you would like to experience this next week.

_____

_____

_____

_____

■ Week 41: It's Not What I Thought

I have been using the same district-assigned textbook for many years. Today I started with an activity in the textbook that I had never tried before because I thought it would be perfect for what I wanted the students to learn. However, when the class was not even halfway through, I had to stop because the activity was not working. On the spot, I had to create a new activity.

While it was frustrating, I realized that I had been relying too much on the textbook to provide what I needed for my lessons each day. I learned that it's not so difficult to let go of something that doesn't work, but it is much harder to randomly create something that does.

I also learned that I had to let go of the fact that the book doesn't always work. I could have allowed my frustration with the book to become a barrier to teaching and learning but in letting go, my students and I could move on efficiently and successfully.

There are times when even a well-prepared lesson doesn't work for one reason or another. Oftentimes, willingness to recognize this and shift in the moment creates a more effective lesson and fosters better learning!

What comes up for you when you see students struggling to understand? Are you willing to stop a lesson and adjust? Or do you prefer to plow through a lesson that is not working because you think it might be better than "causing" chaos by changing the lesson on the fly? What consequences could this have on learning? What shifts are you willing to try when your lessons don't feel like they are flowing properly?

_____

_____

_____

_____

_____

_____

Week 41

Weekly Positivity Chart: Use this chart daily to track your feelings so you get a better idea of what challenges you and what brings you joy. This will support you in changing your habits, nurturing and nourishing yourself, while also improving your impact on your students!

Every morning, I invite you to write down:

One wish you have for yourself today based on a challenge you experienced yesterday.

Every evening, I invite you to write down:

One positive memory from the day in your teaching and/or your personal life that can support you in knowing you are in the right place.

Day 1

AM: _____

PM: _____

Day 2

AM: _____

PM: _____

Day 3

AM: _____

PM: _____

Day 4

AM: _____

PM: _____

Day 5

AM: _____

PM: _____

Day 6

AM: _____

PM: _____

Day 7

AM: _____

PM: _____

Congratulations!
You've completed one week!

Setting your intention for your next week can make a big difference for you and your students!

Envision and describe how you would like to experience this next week.

_____

_____

_____

_____

▉ Week 42: Student Leaders

I had a student who was often loud, angry, and frustrated. When they talked everyone listened because it was hard not to. They talked at inappropriate times about anything and everything. While sometimes they used their energy and knowledge to answer questions, they often answered without being called upon.

Some students were getting frustrated while others were egging them on because it meant they could avoid their work, too.

From the outside, it looked like this student was a negative student leader and that they were creating tension which wasn't benefiting them or anyone else. In reality, it was a wakeup call to me that something needed to shift. I decided to work with the disruption rather than fighting it.

One morning, I gently asked this student to join me in the hallway. I complimented them on their desire to answer questions, the quality of some of their contributions, and the enthusiasm they brought to the class. I then asked if they would be interested in being a positive leader for the class by being responsible for a few tasks. They were at first surprised, then eager, and then proud. This student now checks homework daily, tracks who has had a turn to answer questions, and reminds everyone at the end of the period what the homework is for the evening. They have stopped talking at inappropriate times, the class atmosphere is calmer, and learning is happening!

The student was needing positive attention and didn't know how to get it. Offering a position of leadership, not only boosted self-esteem but also trust. Moreover, I now have more of the support I need, this student has a new sense of belonging and pride, and the other students are able to feel safe as things have become more predictable. What a victory!

How can you promote student leadership as one way to shift rising chaos to peace and collaboration?

_____

_____

_____

Week 42

Weekly Positivity Chart: Use this chart daily to track your feelings so you get a better idea of what challenges you and what brings you joy. This will support you in changing your habits, nurturing and nourishing yourself, while also improving your impact on your students!

Every morning, I invite you to write down:
One wish you have for yourself today based on a challenge you experienced yesterday.

Every evening, I invite you to write down:
One positive memory from the day in your teaching and/or your personal life that can support you in knowing you are in the right place.

Day 1
AM: _____

PM: _____

Day 2
AM: _____

PM: _____

Day 3
AM: _____

PM: _____

Day 4
AM: _____

PM: _____

Day 5

AM: _____

PM: _____

Day 6

AM: _____

PM: _____

Day 7

AM: _____

PM: _____

Congratulations!
You've completed one week!

Setting your intention for your next week can make a big difference for you and your students!

Envision and describe how you would like to experience this next week.

_____

_____

_____

_____

■ Week 43: Embracing Student Talents

This year my classroom feels extra special because I was the lucky recipient of two art students requesting that I be their project mentor for their art graduation requirement.

One of these students painted the monster air conditioning unit. (I know not all schools have AC. This particular school district used bond money for that specific purpose to foster learning.) The other student painted the classroom door and cabinets.

I teach languages and they had fabulous ideas! I now have flags from 10 different countries all over the AC unit and the cabinets. The classroom door says "welcome" in three languages. Not only am I welcoming others into my room, but I now feel welcome, too!

I love my classroom and these students get to see their talent on display! Even though this is a graduation requirement for them, mentoring is a beautiful way to honor them, get to know them, and celebrate their talents. Every year for Back-to-School night and open house, parents and other students get to enjoy the art of these talented students.

You may have a beautiful opportunity for students to feel seen and heard, thus raising their self-esteem. How can you honor and celebrate the talents of your students? What can you weave into your curriculum to offer a positive spotlight on individual students?

_____

_____

_____

_____

_____

_____

▌ Week 43

Weekly Positivity Chart: Use this chart daily to track your feelings so you get a better idea of what challenges you and what brings you joy. This will support you in changing your habits, nurturing and nourishing yourself, while also improving your impact on your students!

Every morning, I invite you to write down:

One wish you have for yourself today based on a challenge you experienced yesterday.

Every evening, I invite you to write down:

One positive memory from the day in your teaching and/or your personal life that can support you in knowing you are in the right place.

Day 1

AM: _____

PM: _____

Day 2

AM: _____

PM: _____

Day 3

AM: _____

PM: _____

Day 4

AM: _____

PM: _____

Day 5

AM: _____

PM: _____

Day 6

AM: _____

PM: _____

Day 7

AM: _____

PM: _____

Congratulations!
You've completed one week!

Setting your intention for your next week can make a big difference for you and your students!

Envision and describe how you would like to experience this next week.

_____

_____

_____

_____

■ Week 44: An Amazing Outcome

One year, I allowed a student to take an exam during lunch because they needed to leave prior to our class period. As it turned out, the student's parents did not pick them up as early as expected, so they ended up coming to class anyway.

At the beginning of the period, I gave students 10 minutes for some last-minute review in small groups. While helping a student at my desk, I overheard the student who had already taken the exam, telling some of their classmates specific things to study. I immediately pulled them aside and let them know that this was considered cheating, therefore they would receive a zero on the test. They were surprised and just as they were about to argue with me, the office came to get them because their parents had arrived.

The next day, I was called into a meeting with the vice principal, the student, and their parents. It was not easy for the parents or their student because they were of the opinion that it was "just minor cheating". However, my vice-principal and I agreed that cheating is cheating and this needed to be addressed. Hearing this, the parents wanted their student pulled out of my class. This wasn't an option because there was no other teacher. So, we all had to agree to disagree and discuss how to move forward. I was confident that the student would do well despite the setback, and assured the parents that if the student kept up on their work, there was no reason they couldn't achieve a high score in the class.

A year later, the parents saw me and shared how pleased they were that I had stood up for integrity. They apologized for giving me a hard time. The parents saw the ways in which the experience empowered their student to take ownership of their mistake. For me, this was such a beautiful reminder that standing in my values was not only important to do but also benefited the student body as a whole.

Every parent and student is not going to agree with us or even like us, and that is okay. Even if many of our students like us we may still have a parent or student who questions us, our teaching style, and our grading process. This is normal. In fact, questioning, when done respectfully, is also good for us. It keeps us honest and effective.

Our students truly thrive when we are willing to uphold academic integrity and an amazing outcome generally occurs!

When have you felt strongly about a decision you made while teaching and stuck to it? Create a list of the academic, social, and personal values that are important to you and how you would like to honor those for yourself and for your students. What is the benefit of you becoming consistent in the way you stand by your values?

_____

_____

_____

_____

_____

_____

_____

_____

_____

_____

_____

_____

_____

Week 44

Weekly Positivity Chart: Use this chart daily to track your feelings so you get a better idea of what challenges you and what brings you joy. This will support you in changing your habits, nurturing and nourishing yourself, while also improving your impact on your students!

Every morning, I invite you to write down:
One wish you have for yourself today based on a challenge you experienced yesterday.

Every evening, I invite you to write down:
One positive memory from the day in your teaching and/or your personal life that can support you in knowing you are in the right place.

Day 1
AM: _____

PM: _____

Day 2
AM: _____

PM: _____

Day 3
AM: _____

PM: _____

Day 4
AM: _____

PM: _____

Day 5

AM: _____

PM: _____

Day 6

AM: _____

PM: _____

Day 7

AM: _____

PM: _____

Congratulations!
You've completed one week!

Setting your intention for your next week can make a big difference for you and your students!

Envision and describe how you would like to experience this next week.

_____

_____

_____

_____

■ Week 45: I Am Prepared

We cannot predict how our students will feel when they enter the classroom, what news there will be in the world impacting each and every one of us, or whether what we prepared for the day will be as effective as we had hoped.

What I know is that as long as I take the time to prepare mentally and academically, I have a sense of calm in my heart, mind, and body which will permeate the room. If I have to flex because of the aforementioned unknowns, it will be okay because I enter the room with the best of intentions.

When we choose to have a steady regimen of planning, it is not just for us but for our students. While I trust my ability to teach anything anywhere at any time, I also know that there is more to teaching than just presenting the information. Our students need us to be mentally and academically prepared so they can feel our calm, too. When we model co-regulation, the ability to manage attention and emotions, it becomes easier for our students to do this as well.

How does it feel when you have not prepared yourself mentally? What do you notice is the difference? Can you feel it in your body? For me, I feel anxious, a twang in my gut, and have even had the feeling that something was going to go wrong. Guess what? It did! What would it look like to trust what your body is telling you? What would it take to center yourself prior to starting your day or your next class?

_____

_____

_____

_____

_____

_____

▌Week 45

Weekly Positivity Chart: Use this chart daily to track your feelings so you get a better idea of what challenges you and what brings you joy. This will support you in changing your habits, nurturing and nourishing yourself, while also improving your impact on your students!

Every morning, I invite you to write down:

One wish you have for yourself today based on a challenge you experienced yesterday.

Every evening, I invite you to write down:

One positive memory from the day in your teaching and/or your personal life that can support you in knowing you are in the right place.

Day 1

AM: _____

PM: _____

Day 2

AM: _____

PM: _____

Day 3

AM: _____

PM: _____

Day 4

AM: _____

PM: _____

Day 5

AM: _____

PM: _____

Day 6

AM: _____

PM: _____

Day 7

AM: _____

PM: _____

Congratulations!
You've completed one week!

Setting your intention for your next week can make a big difference for you and your students!

Envision and describe how you would like to experience this next week.

_____

_____

_____

_____

■ Week 46: Duck, Duck, Goose

No, I didn't sit in a circle every day with my high schoolers playing "Duck, Duck, Goose" (I wish I could have!). However, on many days, I did find a way to add play into the classroom for at least a few minutes. What is the value of play when we have so much curriculum to cover? And what can play look like?

Play is important because it helps us develop cognitively, physically, socially, and emotionally. Play in the classroom allows all of us to access our creativity and practice balancing life and work. Play can come in many forms. It can be body movement, jokes related to your subject, a moment for music, and even dance. It can also be a game, whether you use online sources like WordWall or Kahoot, or adapt a board game to your subject area. Play can also be improvisation.

There are so many ways to engage your learners other than lectures, tests, and homework. However, homework can be fun, too! For example, my students were learning to conjugate regular verbs in Spanish. Instead of the normal boring way of explaining things, I encouraged them to make rap/song videos to teach their verbs concept. They were awesome!

What I have learned is that when I take the time to play in my own life, I am much more welcoming and at ease around play in the classroom. And, when I offer time to play in the classroom, my students are much more welcoming of learning and the overall ambience is joyful!

What is one fun thing you can add to your lesson today or this week? Can you imagine the impact this could have on your overall connection to your students as well as on their learning? What have you got to lose?

_____

_____

_____

_____

_____

▌Week 46

Weekly Positivity Chart: Use this chart daily to track your feelings so you get a better idea of what challenges you and what brings you joy. This will support you in changing your habits, nurturing and nourishing yourself, while also improving your impact on your students!

Every morning, I invite you to write down:

One wish you have for yourself today based on a challenge you experienced yesterday.

Every evening, I invite you to write down:

One positive memory from the day in your teaching and/or your personal life that can support you in knowing you are in the right place.

Day 1

AM: _____

PM: _____

Day 2

AM: _____

PM: _____

Day 3

AM: _____

PM: _____

Day 4

AM: _____

PM: _____

Day 5

AM: _____

PM: _____

Day 6

AM: _____

PM: _____

Day 7

AM: _____

PM: _____

Congratulations!
You've completed one week!

Setting your intention for your next week can make a big difference for you and your students!

Envision and describe how you would like to experience this next week.

_____

_____

_____

_____

Week 47: The Sun Is Out

Sunshine could be a curse or a blessing, a gift, or a challenge. Generally, my students show up feeling happier and active when the weather is sunny. In fact, I also show up feeling happier. When we all show up this way, the energy in the classroom feels really good. Sometimes this leads to better receptivity and more learning...and sometimes it leads to chaos!

What are your experiences with good weather and learning? If you have good classroom management skills and a routine set up, you may not even notice the shift. However, every once in a while, our students can surprise us by being extra squirrely. And, if you have not established solid classroom management, this kind of weather day can really throw you for a loop! So, what do we do?

What has worked for me on days when I notice a bit of extra energy in the classroom is offering five minutes of "free time," "chit chat time," or "game time" at the end of the period, on the condition that everyone stays on task. This keeps us all rooted in learning and allows us to celebrate the joy of warm weather!

Being prepared for this kind of shift can be extremely helpful in maintaining classroom management and supporting learning.

Do you already have something in place for days when there may be more distractions than others? If so, are you willing to share that with a new teacher or another teacher who is struggling? If you do not, take a few moments today to set this up or ask a colleague or two what they have set up. Write those down here so you have them to return to when needed.

_____

_____

_____

_____

_____

_____

▌Week 47

Weekly Positivity Chart: Use this chart daily to track your feelings so you get a better idea of what challenges you and what brings you joy. This will support you in changing your habits, nurturing and nourishing yourself, while also improving your impact on your students!

Every morning, I invite you to write down:
One wish you have for yourself today based on a challenge you experienced yesterday.

Every evening, I invite you to write down:
One positive memory from the day in your teaching and/or your personal life that can support you in knowing you are in the right place.

Day 1
AM: _____

PM: _____

Day 2
AM: _____

PM: _____

Day 3
AM: _____

PM: _____

Day 4
AM: _____

PM: _____

Day 5

AM: _____

PM: _____

Day 6

AM: _____

PM: _____

Day 7

AM: _____

PM: _____

Congratulations!
You've completed one week!

Setting your intention for your next week can make a big difference for you and your students!

Envision and describe how you would like to experience this next week.

_____

_____

_____

_____

■ Week 48: What Inspires Me?

As you approach the end of the year do you find that you struggle to get up in the morning, especially on Mondays? It's like in the movie, Groundhog Day, where almost everything seems to be repeating itself: the school schedule, the same students with their same complaints, the same administrators with their same staff meetings, the same subject you've been teaching all year... When this happens, what inspires you? How do you convince yourself that getting up and teaching another day is worth it?

Take a moment, right now, to write down all the things that inspired you to become a teacher and what gives you joy in your teaching. Set your timer for five minutes and begin writing...Then come back to read the rest of this page. If you'd like, go back to week 23 to remember even more reasons you chose a teaching career. I would also highly recommend that you take all the reasons you love what you do and create a poster of some kind and place it somewhere for regular viewing.

_____

_____

_____

_____

_____

_____

_____

_____

_____

Great job! How did it feel to write? Did you remember what inspired you to choose teaching as a career? Did any of these help turn your frown upside down?

When you are feeling troubled and need encouragement, you can look to this list for reassurance that you are doing what you love, that the things that cause stress are temporary, and that being a teacher truly has a benefit to you and to your students. I would also highly recommend that you take all the reasons you love what you do and create a poster of some kind and place it somewhere for regular viewing.

Additionally, did you know that mindfulness, gratitude lists, and ongoing reflection help keep us in the moment, offer a healthy perspective, and support optimal health?

Practice these (mindfulness, gratitude, positive affirmations) each day for a few weeks and feel free to pass this exercise on to your students. The impact on your mood may surprise you.

Use the space below to list all your resources for mindfulness and meditation, gratitude and affirmations, as well as perhaps some simple physical exercises you can do like Xi Gong. You may also want to use the space below to journal any difference you notice as a result of implementing these techniques.

_____

_____

_____

_____

_____

_____

_____

_____

Week 48

Weekly Positivity Chart: Use this chart daily to track your feelings so you get a better idea of what challenges you and what brings you joy. This will support you in changing your habits, nurturing and nourishing yourself, while also improving your impact on your students!

Every morning, I invite you to write down:
One wish you have for yourself today based on a challenge you experienced yesterday.

Every evening, I invite you to write down:
One positive memory from the day in your teaching and/or your personal life that can support you in knowing you are in the right place.

Day 1
AM: _____
PM: _____

Day 2
AM: _____
PM: _____

Day 3
AM: _____
PM: _____

Day 4
AM: _____
PM: _____

Day 5

AM: _____

PM: _____

Day 6

AM: _____

PM: _____

Day 7

AM: _____

PM: _____

Congratulations!
You've completed one week!

Setting your intention for your next week can make a big difference for you and your students!

Envision and describe how you would like to experience this next week.

_____

_____

_____

_____

■ Week 49: Grades Are Not the End All

It saddened me to find out that there were students who have never played outside, been to a movie with friends or family, or spent a few hours on a couch or in bed reading for pleasure.

A lot of the students I am talking about didn't do these things because they were constantly playing video games or because they didn't like to do them. Rather, they were so stressed out about getting the best grades and being in the top percentile that they didn't "have time" for fun.

I am a firm believer that grades not only aren't the "end all, be all" but that there are even situations or assignments which need to be negotiated for the sake of a student's mental health or wellbeing.

Besides, the more students can quell their anxiety when they recognize stress creeping in, the more successful they will be overall. For example, we can support our students to be honest about the overwhelm they are feeling and teach them to create a plan with bite-sized steps to complete tasks. BUT this plan needs to include fun and rest! How could you do this?

In what ways do you contribute to your students' focusing on grades rather than the content goal? If you were to create a definition of success which has nothing to do with grades, what would it be? How can you share this with your students and their families? What can you do to support your students and families to expand their definition of success so that your students can still work towards being successful without being grade driven?

_____

_____

_____

_____

_____

Week 49

Weekly Positivity Chart: Use this chart daily to track your feelings so you get a better idea of what challenges you and what brings you joy. This will support you in changing your habits, nurturing and nourishing yourself, while also improving your impact on your students!

Every morning, I invite you to write down:
One wish you have for yourself today based on a challenge you experienced yesterday.

Every evening, I invite you to write down:
One positive memory from the day in your teaching and/or your personal life that can support you in knowing you are in the right place.

Day 1
AM: _____

PM: _____

Day 2
AM: _____

PM: _____

Day 3
AM: _____

PM: _____

Day 4
AM: _____

PM: _____

Day 5

AM: _____

PM: _____

Day 6

AM: _____

PM: _____

Day 7

AM: _____

PM: _____

Congratulations!
You've completed one week!

Setting your intention for your next week can make a big difference for you and your students!

Envision and describe how you would like to experience this next week.

_____

_____

_____

_____

Week 50: Taking Care of Your Feelings

Good morning. How are you today? I invite you to check in and ask yourself this question before you leave for work this morning. If you are already at work, this is a great moment to breathe and ask yourself what you are feeling, and how your mood and energy may affect you and your teaching impact today or this week.

So often as an act of survival, we move past our feelings quickly, sometimes even negating their existence. It's as if we think that to look at them will consume us, never get out from under them, or even push us to crawl back under the covers and hide. Or some may worry that if difficult emotions surface, we may lash out at our loved ones, energetically emit an intensity which could set others off, or simply feel paralyzed.

When I take a moment to ask myself, "How are you today, Misha?" I am offering myself radical self-love. I am giving myself attention where I may not have otherwise received it. I am saying, "I care about you, Misha."

Secondly, I am giving myself permission to acknowledge how I am feeling. I can then create a plan to take care of those feelings, so they do not sneak up later and surprise me or anyone else around me.

It is the best sort of modeling we can offer our students.

Take a moment to consider how this practice could elevate your ability to be present and compassionate with your students, your colleagues, and yourself.

Then, make a plan for taking care of your feelings. You may need a mental health day. Perhaps you can take a half day or a full day to reset yourself, take a bath, walk in nature, sit by the water (river, lake, ocean).

Whatever comes of it, I can assure you that this is necessary mental preparation which supports us being the best teachers we can be.

Write your plan for taking care of your feelings below:

_____

_____

Week 50

Weekly Positivity Chart: Use this chart daily to track your feelings so you get a better idea of what challenges you and what brings you joy. This will support you in changing your habits, nurturing and nourishing yourself, while also improving your impact on your students!

Every morning, I invite you to write down:
One wish you have for yourself today based on a challenge you experienced yesterday.

Every evening, I invite you to write down:
One positive memory from the day in your teaching and/or your personal life that can support you in knowing you are in the right place.

Day 1
AM: _____

PM: _____

Day 2
AM: _____

PM: _____

Day 3
AM: _____

PM: _____

Day 4
AM: _____

PM: _____

Day 5

AM: _____

PM: _____

Day 6

AM: _____

PM: _____

Day 7

AM: _____

PM: _____

Congratulations!
You've completed one week!

Setting your intention for your next week can make a big difference for you and your students!

Envision and describe how you would like to experience this next week.

_____

_____

_____

_____

■ Week 51: Right or Wrong

It is so easy to fall into thinking and acting as if there are only two ways of doing things. And for so long, this is how I approached teaching...until I birthed my first child, and then the second one, and finally the third. My eyes opened to a whole new level of diversity in learning and teaching.

Each of my children, just like my students, received, processed, and provided information differently. And, I experienced varying emotions attached to similar things they said and did. One of them could say, "I hate your rules," and this would hardly affect me at all, while another one could say, "I hate your rules," and this would make me reflect more than usual to consider a compromise. And still another could say, "I hate your rules," and I would find myself questioning my parenting ability.

As a result of my own personal exploration, I have learned that everyone gets to have their reaction to life and maneuver through it, without me having to control any of it. However, noticing these huge differences in my own children helped me become more open to approaching each student with more compassion and potentially with a more flexible mindset.

In the wake of this change, this concept of right or wrong, black or white, all or nothing, has disappeared from most of my experiences. There are so many levels, varieties, shades, sizes, etc. which can produce an outcome and engage a learner. We just need to do our best to stay aware of the boxes in which we try to put ourselves and our students. We need to stay open to shifting how we teach so that we can be even more impactful in positive ways.

What kind of thinker are you? If you tend to go from one extreme of the spectrum to the other, or get stuck in a box, what can you do today to adjust your thinking to try something new?

_____

_____

_____

_____

▌Week 51

Weekly Positivity Chart: Use this chart daily to track your feelings so you get a better idea of what challenges you and what brings you joy. This will support you in changing your habits, nurturing and nourishing yourself, while also improving your impact on your students!

Every morning, I invite you to write down:
One wish you have for yourself today based on a challenge you experienced yesterday.

Every evening, I invite you to write down:
One positive memory from the day in your teaching and/or your personal life that can support you in knowing you are in the right place.

Day 1
AM: _____

PM: _____

Day 2
AM: _____

PM: _____

Day 3
AM: _____

PM: _____

Day 4
AM: _____

PM: _____

Day 5

AM: _____

PM: _____

Day 6

AM: _____

PM: _____

Day 7

AM: _____

PM: _____

Congratulations!
You've completed one week!

Setting your intention for your next week can make a big difference for you and your students!

Envision and describe how you would like to experience this next week.

_____

_____

_____

_____

■ Week 52: Good Grief!

This has generally been an expression to symbolize irritation or surprise. In this case, I am referring not to Charlie Brown, but to actual grief and the benefits of allowing it to be felt.

Grief can come in many forms: Sudden, long-term, grieving one's own physical, professional, or personal changes, grieving the death of family members or friends, grieving the death of students to suicide or accidents, or grieving changes in a community such as the resignation of a well-loved administrator.

When I was going through my divorce, there were a lot of changes happening and I did not realize how much my grief was impacting my behaviors or my composure in the classroom. I wasn't processing it. My way of dealing with it was to bulldoze my way through every day just to get through it...until one day. One of my students was also having a rough day and based on something I did, he yelled at me, "Just because you are going through a divorce doesn't mean you have to be mean to us."

Now, we can all sit here and discuss the definition of "mean" or talk about the way this student challenged me, but that isn't the point. Nor is the point to discuss my intention. The point is about how my lack of self-care impacted him, and others. I was not in the touchy-feely mood they were used to and even came across rather insensitive. This surprised them and he had every right to say something.

Could it have been done a different way? Sure. Did it come across the way it needed to? Yes. It made me think and I realized several things, two of which I will share here:

- When we allow ourselves to feel the emotions that come with grief, we offer ourselves and others the gift of centering and processing. Without this we can unintentionally bring disruptive and even damaging energy into the classroom.

- Students are grieving a lot all the time: Growing up, moving from one grade to another; changing classrooms, switching teachers, and losing friends; seeming success or failure on assignments; family dynamics such as divorce, moving, and myriad other situations. This is something we rarely consider in our everyday interactions because of this misconception that we have to be in "it's business as usual" mode.

I am not suggesting that you stop your lessons every day to address your grief or your students' grief. My suggestion is that you take time to care for yourself and honor your grief before coming into the classroom so that you can arrive in a state of compassionate and unconditional service to your students. Grieving is important and when we take time for it, this can make it a gift.

Where there is deep love and passion, there is deep grief, which means it needs to be honored.

What is your routine prior to arriving at school? How do you honor all of you, your emotions, and your experiences? How do you process your grief? How can you acknowledge the grief your students may be experiencing? What can support you in showing up for yourself so that you can also be present for your students?

_____

_____

_____

_____

_____

_____

_____

_____

▌Week 52

Weekly Positivity Chart: Use this chart daily to track your feelings so you get a better idea of what challenges you and what brings you joy. This will support you in changing your habits, nurturing and nourishing yourself, while also improving your impact on your students!

Every morning, I invite you to write down:

One wish you have for yourself today based on a challenge you experienced yesterday.

Every evening, I invite you to write down:

One positive memory from the day in your teaching and/or your personal life that can support you in knowing you are in the right place.

Day 1

AM: _____

PM: _____

Day 2

AM: _____

PM: _____

Day 3

AM: _____

PM: _____

Day 4

AM: _____

PM: _____

Day 5

AM: _____

PM: _____

Day 6

AM: _____

PM: _____

Day 7

AM: _____

PM: _____

Congratulations!
You've completed one week!

Setting your intention for your next week can make a big difference for you and your students!

Envision and describe how you would like to experience this next week.

_____

_____

_____

_____

■ Week 53: Today Is a Gift

Yesterday is history, tomorrow a mystery, and today is a gift, that's why they call it the present. So the idea is that we appreciate it for all it's worth! And, while this is truly something to embrace, sometimes it is really hard to get up and start a new day because it feels so rote. So many of the same routines, tasks, and responsibilities start to make teaching relatively boring if we let it.

Recently, I was going through another bout of depression despite all the things I do for my self-care. I meditate. I write my gratitude daily. I take vitamins and medication. I exercise 3-4 days each week. I play the guitar. I call friends. I eat healthily most of the time. And, getting out of bed has felt just like it used to feel when I had to change a dirty diaper. I don't want to do it but if I don't, things will get messier. That was the only thing that was driving me for several days on end, that if I stayed in bed, things would literally fall apart like a diaper with too much shit in it. And who wants that?!!

The truth of the matter is, my condition is my biochemical make-up, so there is very little I can do when the depression hits other than keep getting up and doing all the things that keep me living rather than lying in it. Fortunately, I was able to change my life philosophy to "there ain't no bad day for me" even when it feels awful. I even wrote a song to remind me!

Whether it is biochemical, situational, or seasonal, I have to remind myself that it is temporary. It always has been. Sometimes it lasts longer than other times. But the reality is that this too shall pass. So when I can identify one thing that makes me smile or laugh or simply feel calm, I get to define the day as a good day.

This makes it so much easier to focus on the positives and I end up seeing many more than I would have, had I chosen to define the entire day as "bad." This doesn't mean I dismiss or negate the sad or uncomfortable feelings. I welcome them in and thank them for showing up. Then I move through my daily practices, sometimes faking it, but knowing I will feel serene and joyful again soon.

As we walk through our pain, we exude resilience and confidence. This healthy modeling for our students can be incredibly impactful. So many of them experience difficulties we cannot even imagine and have far fewer tools to deal with them than we do.

Are you willing to redefine your day when it starts to feel heavily negative in order to offer you a pathway into the positive? How can you embrace your present? What are the gifts of today?

_____

_____

_____

_____

_____

_____

_____

_____

_____

_____

_____

_____

_____

_____

Week 53

Weekly Positivity Chart: Use this chart daily to track your feelings so you get a better idea of what challenges you and what brings you joy. This will support you in changing your habits, nurturing and nourishing yourself, while also improving your impact on your students!

Every morning, I invite you to write down:

One wish you have for yourself today based on a challenge you experienced yesterday.

Every evening, I invite you to write down:

One positive memory from the day in your teaching and/or your personal life that can support you in knowing you are in the right place.

Day 1

AM: _____

PM: _____

Day 2

AM: _____

PM: _____

Day 3

AM: _____

PM: _____

Day 4

AM: _____

PM: _____

Day 5

AM: _____

PM: _____

Day 6

AM: _____

PM: _____

Day 7

AM: _____

PM: _____

Congratulations!
You've completed one week!

Setting your intention for your next week can make a big difference for you and your students!

Envision and describe how you would like to experience this next week.

_____

_____

_____

_____

You Did It! One Full Year Plus!

Hello again you, kind-hearted & loving teacher!

As you come to the end of this book-led journey, I hope it has provided you with some insight and strategies to begin becoming the teacher you are wanting to be. And no, it will not feel perfect. You cannot be perfect. So, I invite you to continue to accept your imperfectness and the imperfectness of your students and colleagues as gifts to each other's ever-growing worlds.

Teaching is not a profession anyone should take lightly. There are so many facets and it's definitely a curvy road. There is nothing that will go exactly like we plan or envision every minute of every day because too many elements can shift it all. However, if we choose to embrace change, this career will be a rewarding, enlightening, and exciting experience. This you can be sure of!

There is more journaling space below for you to write about your favorite parts of the year and identify ways in which you have seen yourself blossom. I also invite you to write one intention that you would like to set for your next year of teaching. Finally, I would like to encourage you to spend time in positive reflection and then fill these pages with love and compassion for you, a radiant teacher!

_____

_____

_____

_____

_____

_____

_____

Don't forget to register your book:

Register your book and receive 12 theme-based meditations, which I created for you to use either daily, weekly, or monthly.

This is a special gift just for people who have purchased or been gifted this book.

You will have access to these meditations in audio form as well as in written transcription.

You just need to go to my website and register your book. The recordings and written transcriptions are free for you.

Go to the following link below to register your book:

https://ceeq.org/shop/p/register-your-purchase

In solidarity and with love,

Misha Safran, PCC, MA
Author, Speaker, Facilitator, and, Teacher